A SHIP TOO FAR

A SHIP TOO FAR
THE MYSTERY OF THE DERBYSHIRE

Dave Ramwell
and
Tim Madge

Hodder & Stoughton
LONDON SYDNEY AUCKLAND

British Library Cataloguing in Publication Data

Ramwell, Dave
  A Ship Too Far: The Mystery of the
  'Derbyshire'
  I. Title   II. Madge, Tim
  363.12

  ISBN 0-340-56997-2

Published by Hodder and Stoughton,
a division of Hodder and Stoughton Limited,
Mill Road, Dunton Green, Sevenoaks, Kent TN13 2YA
Editorial Office: 47 Bedford Square, London WC1B 3DP

Typeset by Rowland Phototypesetting Limited,
Bury St Edmunds, Suffolk
Printed in Great Britain by St Edmundsbury Press Limited,
Bury St Edmunds, Suffolk

'For those in peril on the sea'

To the crew and families of
MV *Derbyshire*
and to all who daily face the
rigours of the world's oceans

Contents

Acknowledgments

This book would not have been written without the help of Peter Ridyard, Nautical Surveyor (now retired), and father of David, lost in the *Derbyshire*. We hope we have done justice, reflecting the tireless patience and tenacity in his quest for truth.

We would like to thank also the following people for their assistance and encouragement:

Billy Anderson (Assistant Shipping Branch Organiser, Liverpool) and all at RMT, Jim Slater CBE (retired President of the National Union of Seamen), Captain E. H. Beetham FNI, Doug Foy (marine journalist and retired Deputy Secretary of Nautical Institute), John Jubb (welding consultant), C. H. Milsom (Editor, *Sea Breezes*), Donald Bilton (retired senior research officer with British Steel Corporation), Malcolm Wright (Tyne Tees *Northern Eye* TV producer), *Derbyshire* Families Association members – especially Cathie Musa, Margaret Noblett, Ros Blease, Ellen Burke, Marion Baylis, Frank Williamson, Paul Lambert, Jim and Freda Kane and Norma Sutton – all those Merchant Navy Association members who rendered valuable assistance, Professor Geraint Price, Dr P. Temarel, Captain C. Penberthy, David Swift (retired Lloyd's Register Surveyor), Hon. Eddie Loyden MP, Hon. Bob Parry MP, Sir Fergus Montgomery MP, all those past members of the *Derbyshire* crews who replied to our letters, Captain Andy Niblock, D. J. Macdonald (Chief Engineer), Rev. Canon Ken Peters and Rev. Peter McGrath.

Dave Ramwell would like to thank his wife Julie for her uncomplaining acceptance of the book's call upon his time, his colleagues on the ship who have had to endure his obsession and one-fingered typing sounding through the alleyway, and last, but by no means least, Tim Madge who made it all happen.

Finally, on behalf of all concerned seafarers, we salute the memory of Professor Bishop, late Vice Chancellor of Brunel University – a true friend to us all.

Introduction

This is the story of a ship – and the reasons why she sank. Conventionally we think of ships sinking through bad weather or collision. Occasionally sinkings are deliberate. But we believe the MV *Derbyshire*, the biggest single loss on the British ship register, suffered from flaws now thought to affect other ships like her. The crucial fact is that when she met extreme weather for the first time she sank, drowning forty-four people.

The story of the *Derbyshire* and her five sister ships is that of the decline of the British merchant navy, and of British shipbuilding too. The *Derbyshire* stands also as a symbol of some of the more extreme aspects of government policies and of slipping standards in British industry. It is not a happy story.

When the *Derbyshire* and her sisters were designed they were the most ambitious class of large vessel ever to be handled by a British yard. For Swan Hunter, then a government-owned company, they represented a great leap in technical accomplishment. The *Derbyshire* was operated safely by her managers, Bibby Line, an old-established shipping company which made its name transporting British soldiers to and from the Empire. But in the commercial pressures of the late 1970s all shipping lines were fighting for a share of a diminishing market. Container ships had arrived with a vengeance, killing off general cargo vessels of which British shipping companies had far too many. And the 'OBO' was much in demand: a ship which could switch cargoes between oil, ore, and bulk goods such as grain. Each of these cargoes is very different in character when loaded or shifting in a heavy sea; and the ships that were designed to carry them are a compromise of vastly different design principles. Such as the *Derbyshire*.

But we believe the *Derbyshire* was not built to the original plans for these giant ships. After the first was built changes were made, which can only be verified today by reference to the sister ships. The plans of how they were in fact built have been mislaid, both by the shipbuilders, Swan Hunter, and by Lloyd's Register.

At the heart of the matter is this question: who authorised a major change in her internal structure? And why cannot the relevant design changes be found, either in Swan Hunter's records or at Lloyd's Register? Of all the thousands of ship design plans on file, these five sets are missing; and it has been argued that no such change was made.

The *Derbyshire* is gone of course, but we have the proof that some of her sister ships were altered, and that it led to continuous and serious problems. The huge and worldwide bulk carrier scandal of 1991 has finally focused attention on the basic issue of bulker design, the same issue that is at the heart of the *Derbyshire* disaster.

The apparent unwillingness to explore, as far as possible, every avenue to find out why she sank may be identified and linked to the twin questions of government money and the credibility of the classification societies in the international shipping market.

First the government. In July 1985, by which time it was apparent that there was a construction defect in sister ships to the *Derbyshire*, the government had privatised Swan Hunter, and in so doing had indemnified the new owners for any claims against ships built in the yard while it was in public hands. It was the government, therefore, that would have to meet the formidable claims not only of the *Derbyshire* but of her sister ships also. These various claims, which included total loss, also involved laying-up time while emergency repairs were carried out.

Secondly, the government was anxious, in our view, not to upset the applecart of British shipping – or shipbuilding. The whole fragile structure was therefore protected against attack – one crucial line of which was, and remains, that safety standards have been slipping and that our former reputation as *primus inter pares* among shipping nations has long been conceded. The arbiters of safety are the classification societies in conjunction with the Department of Transport. Internationally as well as domestically the doyen, Lloyd's Register told the Department of Transport in 1985 that they could not locate the plans for the design changes which, we shall demonstrate, are thought by at least one major academic source to have weakened the *Derbyshire*'s overall structural integrity (see Chapter 13).

Our own involvement is easy to explain. Captain Dave Ramwell is a mariner who worked for the now defunct Palm Line. Like many deep-sea men he finally hung up his sea boots and, if not entirely swallowing the anchor, at least slung his hook in the Mersey, where he skippers a humble sludge boat, *Consortium I*, back and forth, day and night. He came across the *Derbyshire* case by accident and, unlike the majority of 'men of goodwill', he did something, precisely in order that justice may triumph. Dave Ramwell's fight became Tim Madge's when they met during the course of Tim Madge's research for a book on the decline of Britain as a maritime nation.

Tim Madge believed then, as now, that this extraordinary story should be told to as wide an audience as possible. Together we have tried in this book to do that.

This story of a ship is also the story of a few men and women, relatives of the crew of the *Derbyshire*, who have kept the issue alive. Among them Cathie Musa and Peter Ridyard stand out. It is hard to reflect their innate sense of injustice, and their determination to get to the facts. As we write, the findings of the formal inquiry published in 1989 still stand – that the ship was 'probably' lost to bad weather.

The loss of the *Derbyshire* was in its way as bad a disaster as that of the *Titanic* or of the *Herald of Free Enterprise*, though both of those were passenger ships and the *Derbyshire* was a workhorse, a bulker, and she was lost far away in the Pacific. Yet we believe her loss will stand in future years for a change for the better in international shipping. Today, in 1992, what the relatives of the crew want more than money is to know that their menfolk, and the two wives on board, did not die for nothing.

Part 1

Voyages Too Far?

1

The Last Hours of the *Derbyshire*

There is no first-hand account of the sinking of the *Derbyshire*. In the short reconstruction which follows we have used our imagination to describe her death agonies. The details of her life however are factual.

As dawn broke on the morning of September 9th, 1980 two hundred miles east-north-east of Okinawa, the fury of the storm could at last be gauged by the men on the bridge of the Derbyshire. *The seas were wild and confused, a product of the storm 'Orchid' having 'recurved', turned back on itself, during the hours of darkness. Captain Underhill, master of the* Derbyshire, *was worried. As he stared through the gloom he could see, eight hundred feet away across the angry seas breaking across his deck, the bow of the* Derbyshire *lifting to the enormous waves, thirty feet, sometimes forty feet from trough to crest. The ship felt sluggish, unhappy in her movements.*

He had ordered his Chief Officer, 'Curly' Baylis, to keep the ship headed, as far as possible, into the predominant wave direction, effectively heaving-to until daylight gave them a better idea of what they faced. Now he determined to radio Bibbys once more, his owners in Liverpool, to give them a revised time of arrival in Japan. One thing alone made him feel less anxious. With 157,000 tons of iron ore loaded in seven of the Derbyshire's *nine holds, at least there could be little fear of the cargo shifting. He turned from staring into the murk, announced to his Chief his intentions, and walked off the bridge.*

The Derbyshire *was so large that, even under these conditions, the pitching and rolling high up on the superstructure was not so bad that he had to grab at any handhold. Despite his concern off Cape Town she was, after all, a giant of a ship, secure in any weather.*

If Captain Underhill's worries that day centred on whether his ship would be late into Japan, then some of his crew were less sanguine. To them this storm was taxing their ship beyond endurance. The Derbyshire *carried forty-two officers and crew – and two wives. For Ronnie Musa, Liverpool seaman of long standing, the noises the ship was making that fateful day brought back disturbing memories of his former ship-mate – another Ronnie – Kan, the cook. Kan had been so bothered by what he described as the* Derbyshire's *propensity to 'cry' in a heavy sea that he had insisted*

[3]

on being paid off on an earlier voyage, even though it had meant finding his own air fare home. Kan had been upset by the death of his mother-in-law, and his wife's reaction to it. It had preyed on his mind, and the ship's terrible screaming, 'like something tightening up', had made his life impossible. When he went, so did two others, equally bothered by the noises.

Others still aboard had remarked on the ship's 'jinxed' existence, some believing, as seaman Jim Noblett did, that it had started when two men were killed in an engine room explosion on the ship's maiden voyage. There had been more recent problems, for example a forward deck plate had come right off in bad weather. Ronnie Kan insists today that 'the ship was rotting. In the galley you were scared to scrub down because so much rust was coming through.' He says that the ship was continually being sandblasted at sea to keep the rust on deck and on her sides to a minimum, although to at least one other of the ex-crew this did not indicate anything unusual.

The Derbyshire *was, however, a happy ship. Officers and crew had their own messes, but in normal conditions they met socially once a week to play darts. The accommodation was good, each man had his own cabin with a shower; and wives could join their menfolk, as on this trip. Some had done so more than once.*

On this day the two women were below, unwilling to watch the ship as she struggled with the storm. Both Anne-Marie Hutchinson, wife of Graeme, the Third Engineer, and Mary Jones, wife of David, Second Engineer, were very bothered by the bad weather, despite the ship's size. Both remembered that Captain Underhill had mentioned that the ship had had problems in the area just forward of the superstructure, although, as he had said, experts had told him these would not affect the ship. In any case it had been surveyed and passed in Japan in April. The experts who had been consulted at the time had dismissed his concern, pointing out that cracking on ships of this size was common.

The facts about the *Derbyshire's* life before this last tragic voyage are well-documented in official papers. She was relatively new, the last of a series of six ships built by Swan Hunter in their Haverton Hill yard on Teesside, dating from the early to mid-1970s. She was launched as the *Liverpool Bridge* in 1976 and changed her name to *Derbyshire* in 1977 (see page 46). All the six ships of the class were designed to be OBOs – oil-bulk-ore carriers – and were the biggest ships of their kind in the world at the time they were launched. They were the biggest Swan Hunter had ever built. Their purpose in the increasingly competitive international shipping market of the 1970s was to combine economy of size with flexibility of use. By necessity they were complex ships to run.

But the *Derbyshire* had not been in commission for all of her short life. Between 1978 and 1979 she was laid up in Stavanger in Norway, a victim of the longest shipping slump in memory. When reactivated in April 1979 she was switched by her owners, Bibby Line, from bulk cargoes to carrying oil. But at the beginning of 1980 she was switched again to dense bulk cargoes – ore and coal. It was then that the cracking began forward of the superstructure, at a point known as Frame 65. By April 1980 it was bad enough for urgent repairs during a routine drydocking in Sasebo, Japan, when the welds along Frame 65 were 'veed out' and strengthened. At the same time shell-plating damage was also repaired. This had included a fracture of the starboard bilge keel.

It had been something of a surprise to the Sasebo yard that they had had as much to do as this. The *Derbyshire* was a young ship and this was already her second drydocking. The first had been in Setenave in Portugal in June and July 1977.

The Lloyd's report,[1] issued after Sasebo on April 17th, 1980, had recommended that the *Derbyshire* be credited her annual and drydocking surveys, and suggested a postponement of her special survey until some time before April 1981. Her hatch covers had been tested (with hoses) for watertightness, her four lifeboats had been serviced and the 'falls' were renewed in each. The ship was in effect issued a temporary certificate, with the recommendation that a special survey be completed within a year. These 'special' surveys are normal practice among the world's classification societies, and are meant to ensure that ship's standards are met for whatever cargoes they are authorised to carry.

She then sailed from Japan to Australia where she loaded coal for France. From the port of Fos-sur-Mer, close to Marseilles, she was joined by her final crew flown there from Liverpool, and sailed to Canada to load iron ore at Sept Iles. Her last voyage began on July 11th, 1980.

The *Derbyshire* was eased from her berth in Sept Iles to begin the 11,000 mile journey across the Atlantic and Indian Oceans, past the Cape of Good Hope, to Japan. Throughout the voyage she was weather-routed by Ocean Routes Inc. of California, a highly automated, satellite-based service designed to keep ships clear of any really bad weather.

Tropical revolving storms – hurricanes and typhoons – are common to certain regions of the world in certain seasons. Like the equinoctial gales off the coasts of Europe, they pose a threat on land and at sea. Over the years seafarers have evolved increasingly better techniques to avoid them altogether or, if caught on the edge of one, to sail clear. From the late 1970s satellite weather services were available to masters of any ship of size, providing constantly up-dated information on the whereabouts of a tropical storm and how it was moving.

Captain Underhill, an experienced master mariner, not only knew what a tropical storm was, he also knew how not to get caught in one. On September 10th, 1980 despite the force of the wind and waves he felt satisfied that he had outwitted even the recurving of storm Orchid. As he made his way from the bridge, in his mind he detected a slight easing of the winds howling across the superstructure compared with an hour or so ago. Although the seas were still dangerous, his skill and that of his officers had ensured that the Derbyshire *had lain bow-to in the worst of the breaking seas.*

Yet even if the ship had been beam-on (sideways to the prevailing seas), he was sure they would have been able to cope. All nine massive hatch covers on the exposed deck had remained firmly shut, and iron ore, as he had often pointed out to his fellow-mariners, had the great advantage in bad weather of holding a big ship firmly down. Unlike some of his professional colleagues, he believed this to be of greater importance than the other characteristic of ore – making the ship 'stiff' and giving her a more rapid return to the upright when she rolled. He was convinced it was this tendency that was making her 'cry', as Ronnie Kan used to put it, on this particular day. He paused on the way to his day cabin, where he would write the log and compose his radio message, to feel his ship lift to another huge rolling wave. There! he thought. Hardly any pitch at all.

Then there came a noise like no man or woman on board had ever heard before. It was an ear-splitting bang, impossibly high-pitched, a shrieking, screaming sound, shocking in its suddenness and its message. On the bridge Curly Baylis, in complete astonishment, saw a dark line run from port to starboard across 145 feet of deck in an instant. His ship had split in two. Almost at once the superstructure began to tilt aft, away from the deck, as a giant wave rolled under the Derbyshire. *There was a rumbling thud far below and Baylis knew the keel, the one element of the* Derbyshire *that ran from end to end, had snapped.*

The giant wave passed under the bridge, and in its trough the top-heavy and now completely detached superstructure was tipped forward into the space growing between it and the rest of the ship. The forward part of the Derbyshire *now swung to port and the superstructure capsized instantly, tilting fast to starboard as it did so. As the next huge wave thundered past the still floating forward two-thirds of the ship, it swept over the entire superstructure, dragging it under.*

The fore part was awash by now, due to the weight of the iron ore cargo.

The destruction of the biggest ship ever lost on the British register had taken less than a minute.

What we have dramatised here cannot be proved. But we know something of the *Derbyshire's* career and the characters of her crew; and we know the facts about parallel disasters involving bulk carriers, especially the *Derbyshire's* sister ships. The issue – and our purpose in this book – is to examine the available evidence about the birth, life and death of the *Derbyshire's* class of ships, and to tell for the first time the complete story.

By 1991 a major international shipping crisis had developed over the building, operation – and losses – of bulk carriers over the world's oceans. The growing losses of this one type of ship had profound financial implications for shipbuilders, owners, insurers and the classification societies such as Lloyd's Register of Shipping. Many lives had been lost; hundreds of millions of pounds in insurance and compensation money had been paid out. Yet the ships were sinking in regular, frequently unexplained circumstances, involving over 300 seamen and 200 bulk carriers in the ten years since the *Derbyshire* was lost. In the eighteen months from 1990 to autumn 1991 alone, forty bulkers were lost or seriously damaged (almost one every fortnight). Yet scientific evidence, which could have helped to save some of these ships, was at least 'known about' from the time the *Derbyshire* sank.

On September 10th, 1980 as the *Derbyshire* sank with all hands to the north-east of Okinawa, the outlying islands of Japan, the rest of the world was not unduly anxious about her. The day before, a radio signal from the ship to Bibby Line had stated: VESSEL HOVE TO VIOLENT STORM FORCE 11 WIND NE X E SEAS APPROX 30 FEET OVERCAST CONTINUOUS RAIN PRESSURE 995 MB. Later the *Derbyshire* was in contact with the MV *Alrai*. At the time she reported she was eighty miles ahead of the *Alrai* where the storm was deepest with a barometer of only 962mb and wind force 12 (winds of 65 knots, gusting to perhaps 90 knots). The *Alrai* was experiencing wave heights between sixty and a hundred feet, but these difficult conditions are not impossible for a ship to cope with, as the *Alrai's* survival proves.

Captain Underhill had signalled that he was expecting to arrive in Kawasaki on September 14th, late because of the storm. He was receiving constantly up-dated weather information. On September 9th storm Orchid was known to be 130 miles from the last reported position of the *Derbyshire* and to her south-east, heading at a forward speed of 14 knots to the north-west.

Every official report published has referred extensively to Orchid as a cause of the loss of the *Derbyshire*, and therefore it is worth looking into its progress in some detail. At the official inquiry in 1987–8[2] it was stated:

Typhoon Orchid was an unusual tropical revolving storm both in regard to its behaviour south of Japan (high speed cyclonic loops) and its large size. It originated in the waters north of the Caroline Islands around Guam, some 1000 miles east of the Philippines in an area near the eastern extension of the monsoon trough . . . On September 6th satellite imagery indicated that a tropical cyclone formation alert was required for this rapidly developing disturbance . . . a gale warning was issued. The first warning . . . was issued on September 7th.

It was a tropical storm heading west-north-westwards. By the following day, after crossing the 20th parallel near 136°East, it began the familiar parabolic curve northwards but never completely recurved. By September 9th Orchid developed to typhoon strength and on the 10th winds had increased to 85 knots (about 100 mph). Typhoon Orchid moved across Kyushu on September 11th and dropped to tropical storm strength as she moved across the Sea of Japan.

During September 9th and 10th Orchid executed three high speed loops while maintaining an overall forward speed of about 14 knots northwards. This movement is not clearly apparent from the radio warnings issued at the time . . .

The report suggests that Captain Underhill was trying to pass ahead of the path of the storm, predicting its behaviour from what his experience told him it was likely to do. The implication with reference to 'high speed loops' is that Underhill – and hence the *Derbyshire* – was caught out. All revolving tropical storms have a 'safe' and a 'dangerous' semicircle. The view of the Wreck Commissioners was that, by guess or by God, Underhill had got it wrong and found himself in the dangerous semicircle of Orchid. But the report says it does not 'impugn' the actions of Captain Underhill.

What is not explained is how the 'forces of nature' actually overwhelmed the *Derbyshire*. A well-built, almost new ship with a reasonable expectation of a working life of twenty years, with her hatches secured, can withstand the most appalling weather. One suggestion out of the blue was that her engines failed. But this would not explain why no more radio messages were sent; neither would any other speculation do so, except for the obvious one: that she suffered such a catastrophic failure that there was no time.

If this was due to a wave, it was some wave, moving at an inordinately high speed. Failure of hatch covers due to such a wave would again suggest a slow enough disaster to allow some distress message to be sent before the ship was overwhelmed – or for some survivors to get away. To posit the failure of all nine covers seems truly unbelievable. Much more believable, in our view, is the sort of structural failure we have dramatised.

It was only on Saturday, September 13th when she failed to arrive in Okinawa that the first effort was made to instigate a search. Although ships will go missing temporarily, it seems obvious now that an attempt ought to have been made sooner to check that the ship had come through Orchid intact. Bibbys, through their Japanese agents, asked the Japanese Maritime Safety Agency to mount a search on that Saturday. The Japanese, however, said that they could not comply until the ship was at least twenty-four hours overdue, which was held to be on September 15th – the day following Captain Underhill's last estimated time of arrival and six days after his last radio contact. The search which began on September 15th was conducted by two patrol vessels, the *Osumi* and the *Motobu*, and two aircraft, numbers 791 and 811. It was one of the aircraft from the agency which spotted an oil slick about twenty miles to the north-east of the *Derbyshire's* last known position. The *Osumi* subsequently confirmed oil rising to the surface at the point the aircraft had indicated, forming a mile-long slick. There were no other signs of a lost ship, and the search was suspended on September 17th as another tropical storm, 'Sperry', was threatening the area. A resumption, for one day, found no further signs of the ship or her crew, although more oil was spotted of which a sample was later shown to be compatible with fuel oil used by the *Derbyshire*, and the search was called off in the evening of September 18th.

Six weeks later, on October 24th, the Japanese ship *Taiei Maru*, sailing about 250 miles to the north-east of the search area, came across one of the *Derbyshire's* lifeboats. It was severely damaged, as if it had been wrenched with great force from its davits on the ship. It was empty and the Japanese crew made no attempt to recover it. Yet that lifeboat had a story to tell. Part of the launching tackle was left hanging inside the boat (conventional launching would have left these on the ship). The wire fall ends were all ripped to shreds, consistent with a violent parting from her davits. Damage to the lifeboat hull was consistent too with severe impact and abrasion as she was 'launched'. The evidence is that this lifeboat, the only part of the *Derbyshire* to survive, was torn from her place on the ship's superstructure.

As the after end of the ship sank, separated from the cargo holds and capsized to starboard, it trapped the lifeboat. Then in a few seconds as the port side showed its accommodation windows to that leaden sky, tons of typhoon-driven water rushed across the white topsides between the lifeboat and the deck, bursting it from its stricken host.

On September 22nd, that is, before the lifeboat was sighted, and to the south, another Bibby Line vessel, the *Cambridgeshire*, a bulk carrier *en route* from Japan to Australia, stopped in the approximate position where the *Derbyshire* sank. Her officers and crew conducted a short service and threw wreaths on the water. The *Derbyshire* had been posted at Lloyd's as a missing vessel.

In due course about £11 million was paid, largely by Lloyd's (the London shipping insurers), as an insurance claim. Almost 82 per cent of the insurance had been placed with London underwriters. The value of the iron ore was assessed at $2.6 million, and the hull and machinery at $24 million (about £11 million in 1980). For the relatives – widows mostly – the settlement averaged £5,000 from Bibbys per ordinary crew member (the ratings). For all those families and friends the death of their husbands, brothers, sons and daughters caused terrible heartache, and they are still struggling to understand what happened. These people are the long-term and continuing victims of this shipping disaster. Their fight to get to the bottom of the tragedy is a demonstration of fortitude and personal courage despite, in some cases, desperate poverty.

It began for them all on a sunny Sunday evening, September 14th, 1980, the day the *Derbyshire* was due in Japan. Helen Burke, wife of seaman Tim, was at home:

> We were just sat watching television and someone rang from Bibby to say the ship was missing but not to get alarmed. They said they had to tell us because there might be something on the news about it. They assured me that nothing had happened really so I just went on watching television. Then, believe it or not, I went to Bingo. They all said Tim would be all right but when I came home it was preying on my mind and I remember I got my quilt and pillow and lay down on the couch. The next morning I still couldn't really grasp that anything had happened. The children were in bed, I just got dressed – my sister-in-law lives just along the road and I ran and told her. I'd come back home and was getting the children off to school when it came on the wireless . . .

Ros Blease's husband, Tom, was the 'chippy', the carpenter:

> It was on the Monday [September 15th] and I was working in the shop and a girl came in and started asking questions about the *Derbyshire*. I'd no idea why and then the lady whose shop it was said that there had been something on the radio. So we listened to the next news and it was then that they read out all the names of the men. She rang Bibbys for me then – we weren't on the phone. Later Bibbys said they had sent someone round but I wasn't in . . .

The Last Hours of the Derbyshire

Margaret Noblett's husband, Jim, was a seaman on the ship:

It was the Sunday night. My two small children had gone to bed and I'd taken the dog for a walk. I called at a friend's house for a coffee. I was expecting Jim back on the Tuesday – you start to rush round a bit when you know they are coming home. While I was having my coffee the phone rang; it was my eldest girl, Eileen, who was eighteen then. She said Bibbys had rung and when they found out who she was they asked how old she was. When she said eighteen they had said, 'OK, we can tell you. We haven't heard from the ship for a couple of days.' They said not to worry though, she had been in a typhoon and probably the radio had been damaged. They were ringing because there might be something in the press and they didn't want folk to worry too much. My friend had been a seaman and he said he'd take me home. Since then I heard he told everyone he knew it was bad news – they would not have heard from the ship for days before making that call. Anyway he brought me home with the dog in the car and said, 'Don't worry.' The next morning I went to work – as a caretaker at a little primary school. I hadn't slept all night and when I opened the school up the headmaster arrived and looked at me and said, 'What's the matter?' When I told him he said he'd take me home. It was then, I think, that I suddenly realised what it all meant. I went home and I put my TV on: at one, it was on the news.

Cathie Musa, wife of Ronnie, had heard nothing on the Sunday. On the Monday morning she went shopping:

When I was coming up the road my neighbour across the street shouted to me and said, 'Come here, Cathie,' and I shouted back I had to get home for my daughter's lunch. She said, 'You've time for this,' and I went over and she said, 'Your husband's on the *Derbyshire*, isn't he?' I just froze. She told me there had been something on the radio at twelve o'clock, that his name had been mentioned. I couldn't speak. She took me over the road and told me to get on to Bibbys and I rang them and said, 'What's all this about the *Derbyshire*?' It was Stan Clayton from the personnel department who I got and he said, 'So you didn't get the message, then?' I said, 'No, what would I be getting a message for?' He just said, 'The ship's lost.' I said, 'You've got to be joking, how can you lose a big ship like that?' I remember screaming down the phone at him about not being so bloody stupid, just send someone to look for it. I just went crazy – berserk. I could not believe such a big ship had gone missing . . .

Marion Baylis, whose husband Curly ('we always called him that') was the Chief Officer, has total recall of the night she heard about the loss. 'I am sure I use the same words every time,' she says today:

It was a Sunday night. My daughter, Pam, was seventeen then. I had run her back to college in Northampton and when I got home my sixteen-year-old, Richard, said, 'Bibby Line have rung. They say the ship won't be in Japan tomorrow, she has been delayed. They want you to know about it in case you read it in the papers.' I said, 'That sounds daft.' I am sure we watched *The Last Night of the Proms* even though it was on a Sunday. Looking back I wonder why I didn't telephone Bibby. At the back of my mind I kept thinking, 'They don't work on a Sunday night.' I had a friend who was starting in college and the next morning I rang her to say Curly wouldn't be in Japan that day. Just after I had put the telephone down she rang back and said, 'Marion, it's not what you think it is, put the radio on, quickly.' When I did – it was Radio Two – they said the ship was missing. The children had gone to school by this time so I went round to tell my in-laws. I rushed back – I was scared to stay out of the house for very long in case the telephone rang. It was just terrible because I knew then he would never come back. The house began to fill up with people and I felt very guilty because they said, 'You mustn't give up hope,' and I knew it was no good. You have to understand that Curly and I had started to attend a church because I was lonely. Both of us had found a faith. I used to say my prayers for Curly every night. The previous ten days I had not been able to pray for him – so I knew. They were all saying don't give up, but I had.

These are snapshots, frozen frames from a decade ago but sharply in focus to the women who remember as if it were yesterday. Many of the families have similar stories to tell. And as time passes it seems, to the widows in particular, to have got worse. They feel that time has not healed but rather betrayed their grief.

In the aftermath of September 1980 a lasting tragedy began. For the families and friends of the crew of the *Derbyshire* have had no one to bury.

Each year there is a memorial service in Liverpool; many attend. Others have private ceremonies. Margaret walks along the front at Southport each anniversary of the sinking and looks at the sea, seeking happier thoughts. Cathie until recently took one of the Mersey ferries, the *Royal Iris*, now up for sale. 'They used to stop in the middle of the river for me,' she says, 'just for a moment.' The depth of feeling of these people was perhaps enhanced by the worst of all bereavements – the absence of anyone to bury.

Then, after seven years, in 1987 the public inquiry began, and most of them felt that it would at last bring an end to the darkest of all their nights. What they gained, however, was not peace but anger, principally over the way, as they saw it, that the inquiry did not call evidence which, they sincerely believed, rightly or wrongly, might have helped to solve the mystery of the ship's disappearance. Some of them began to see that there were hundreds of unanswered questions concerning the *Derbyshire* and that she was a class of ship that had encountered problems at sea. Most shocking, to some of them, was the discovery that the *Derbyshire* might have split at Frame 65 and that scientific evidence from unimpeachable academic sources had suggested years before that this was a vulnerable point in all bulkers. Finally they were to learn in detail of the *Kowloon Bridge*, the *Derbyshire's* sister, which had broken up off the Irish coast, splitting at Frame 65 as she sank.

Frame 65 is so important we have given it a whole chapter (Ch. 7) but it would be wrong to think everything hinges on this one section of a massive ship. In the *Derbyshire's* case the risk may have been less to Frame 65 than where this frame lay in the hull – about one-third of the way from the stern. The recent spate of disappearing bulk carriers all over the world in circumstances as mysterious as that of the *Derbyshire* was predicted some years ago. But it was not until October 1990 that an academic paper was published linking the *Derbyshire* to other bulk carrier losses. Meetings at the Royal Institute of Naval Architects (RINA) are not normally known for their dramatic quality. This meeting was more than dramatic: it was sensational.

2

A Theory on the Loss of the *Derbyshire*

Ten years were to pass from the September the *Derbyshire* sank until a highly plausible academic paper on the subject was presented at a public meeting. For more than half that time the families and friends of the crew had no idea there might be a scientific explanation at variance with the findings of the formal inquiry, that the cause was unknown or probably due to bad weather.

By the late 1980s evidence of the large number of bulk carriers which had disappeared in similar circumstances to the *Derbyshire* was overwhelming, as we shall demonstrate. International shipping statistics were becoming dominated by these losses. This, along with a slow but tenacious campaign to get to the bottom of the *Derbyshire* case, was forcing the issue.

The Royal Institute of Naval Architects had invited Professor Geraint Price who, by late 1990, held the chair in Ship Science at Southampton University, to read a paper on the *Derbyshire* and her sister ships. The research, which was prepared in 1984 for the Department of Transport, had been conducted by Professor Bishop of Brunel University and his two colleagues, Geraint Price, then Professor of Applied Mechanics, and Dr Pandeli Temarel, a lecturer at the same university. It therefore had good credentials and was regarded as crucially important in any attempt to establish why such a huge ship as the *Derbyshire* could simply disappear.

The novelty of the Bishop, Price and Temarel paper should not be underestimated. Naval architecture has evolved over centuries rather than years. Shipbuilders, from Noah on, are inherently cautious men. The principles of their craft go back long before Archimedes. As for ship design, the great revolutions of the twentieth century have been the change from riveted ships to welded ones and the inexorable reduction of manning levels on board. Ships have changed their external shape very little; internally – and this is part of the most crucial area of debate – they have been transformed. The big change in bulk carrier design has been towards huge bin-like holds, gigantic hoppers for bulk cargoes, whether liquid, like oil; liquefied, like gas; or solid, like grain and ore (see Chapter 14).

The novelty of the research, then, lies in its concentration on dynamic forces rather than static ones. Simply put, this means looking at what happens when a ship, loaded or not, moves in waves and weather rather than how she behaves when sitting still. Needless to say the mathematics and the analysis are complex. Shipbuilders – and ship classifiers – rely to this day far more, if not exclusively, on static tests. These may involve simply loading a cargo and seeing how a ship lies in the water; they may involve tipping a ship sideways to see how fast she rights herself. They have not involved putting strain gauges along the deck of a ship at sea in a gale. And, to be fair, the methods that have been used have appeared to be successful, in that most ships do not sink, whatever the cargo or weather.

It was perhaps the 'dynamic' approach which attracted so many people to the Weir Hall in October 1990 when the Bishop, Price and Temarel paper was given its first public hearing. Indeed so many people turned up that some were left standing in the doorway. Dave Ramwell attended the meeting, bringing with him, as he always has for some years, his *Derbyshire* 'starter's pack' for any interested party. Sitting near the front he handed one of these to the man sitting next to him.

Fourteen speakers were scheduled to reply to Professor Price's reading of the paper (Professor Bishop had died in 1989). The first four were to be from Lloyd's Register.

Summarised, the paper[1] said this:

Losses of bulk carriers in unexplained circumstances are by no means rare, averaging, it is said, about twenty per annum. The largest British vessel ever lost at sea was the oil-bulk-ore carrier *Derbyshire*, which sank without trace in September 1980. If the reason for the loss of the *Derbyshire* could be established – the exact location of the wreck is not known and so an inspection is out of the question – perhaps a lead would be given to the apparent vulnerability of bulk carriers in general. This paper records a lengthy investigation which was conducted with this aim and which is reported here in two parts.

The first part relates to theoretical studies. These suggest that, although field stresses in the hull of the *Derbyshire* complied with design rules that have not changed significantly to this day, they were in fact dangerously large. The calculations strongly suggest that cracking would most likely occur just forward of the superstructure; a prediction made with far more rudimentary techniques was thus confirmed.

The second part of this paper is based on a re-reading of the available information, bearing in mind that calculations made for the *Derbyshire* are effectively calculations made for her sister ships, of which there were five. The history of all of the six sister ships was examined to see to what extent a pattern of behaviour emerges. Here again the evidence leads to quite firm conclusions.

There turns out to be no serious conflict between the conclusions reached in the two parts of this paper. In the very nature of things neither part can be conclusive but both point in the same direction. It is perhaps arguable, therefore, that the fate of the *Derbyshire* has been established. It is suggested that the conclusions reached have significance for *all* bulk carriers, so that some good may emerge from the tragic loss to which this paper relates.

At bottom, what the research says is that the effect of dynamic stresses in bulkers results in there being two areas in the length of a hull where the build-up of forces may be dangerous. This is in addition to the traditional view that such stress is concentrated in the mid-point of any hull. The Bishop, Price and Temarel research says that at a fifth of the way along a ship's length – bow and stern – stresses will also peak. In the *Derbyshire* 0.2 of the length measured from the stern forward brings us, exactly, to Frame 65. It should be said here that when the academics did their research on the *Derbyshire* specifically, they had no idea that this was an area of concern.

The first efforts to measure such stresses in ships occurred in the 1970s, when the first huge 'Capesize' bulkers – like the *Derbyshire* and her sister ships – were being built. In the original (1984) paper, which was prepared for the Department of Transport after the Bishop, Price team had approached the Department for permission to analyse the *Derbyshire* data, the conclusion was 'reported with some diffidence'. This is not surprising. The researchers were linking failure with fatigue mechanisms in a ship that was only four years old. In actual terms of work, since the *Derbyshire* had been laid up for a year, she was only three years old. It was thus a very radical conclusion indeed. It must be stressed however that the Bishop, Price work remains to this day essentially a theory; but given the circumstances of the growing losses of bulkers we believe, as do others, both interested experts and lay people, that it does offer the vital link between bulk carriers, including the *Derbyshire* and her sister ships, and dynamic stresses experienced at sea.

In the event the Brunel University team found its original research missing from official documents. They were not called to the public inquiry on the loss of the *Derbyshire*, which incidentally took eight years to set up.

The Brunel University team did continue their research, as the RINA paper proves. Although throughout their work and in discussions of it the team has been at pains not to impute any 'blame' for the *Derbyshire's* loss, before he died Professor Bishop told Dave Ramwell that he believed the latest part of the research to be 'devastating' in its implications.

In Weir Hall that October night in 1990 the reading of this paper caused a sensation. Dry academic data suddenly took on the theatrical clothes of the truly dramatic. Its effect on some in that hall was electrifying. The first speaker to reply to Professor Price said, among other things, that 'there can hardly have been a paper read before any technical institution which so utterly failed to meet its objectives as this one has'. The others followed in the same vein. Lloyd's Register, some of whose surveyors had replied at the meeting, subsequently put out a press release dismissing the RINA paper and saying that the research would, if left unchallenged, 'mislead the general public and, more importantly, those distressed by the loss of the *Derbyshire*'.

Some of the speakers were as positively for the paper as the most acrimonious of those against. But it would be wrong to see in the debate that followed the need to 'win' or 'lose'. Professor Price has had a large correspondence since that evening, some of it highly significant, from long-standing experts in ship construction whose own attitudes had been changed by the paper's conclusions.

The issue of how the *Derbyshire* was lost has to be addressed none the less, and we shall do so in detail, as well as discussing the questions surrounding her building by Swan Hunter – and that of her sister ships – and her subsequent career.

The RINA meeting was relied upon by many of the *Derbyshire* campaigners to resolve the issue and some believed it had. They were to be disappointed. The government's position did not change on reopening any inquiry. Malcolm Rifkind, the Minister of Transport, told the House of Commons that a reading of the Bishop Report had not convinced him of any need to reopen the inquiry. The Department of Transport's Chief Maritime Inspector, Captain Peter Marriott, had advised Rifkind in a letter written after this meeting, that Bishop's conclusion for the loss of the *Derbyshire* and her sister ship, *Kowloon Bridge*, was the same: a 'relatively vulnerable' frame structure. He then quoted the necessarily weak last lines of its conclusion: 'We are not entirely without evidence but frankly admit we do not know how the loss occurred.' Indeed how could they? The *Derbyshire* carcass lies in thousands of feet of water.

Marriott's advice to Rifkind was consistent with the conclusions of the inquiry undertaken by the Wreck Commissioner appointed by his Department. The formal inquiry report had not said the *Derbyshire* had sunk because of a 'relatively vulnerable' frame structure (Frame 65). It had eventually dismissed all the evidence of structural failure, saying the ship was lost almost certainly due to bad weather. As far as Frame 65 was concerned, the inquiry had said the design 'in way of Frame 65' was satisfactory.

Yet practices are changing, both in the way ships are surveyed and in the way bulk carriers, at least, are built. In 1991 Harland and Wolff won a contract for six bulk carriers. These ships are to be substantially 'beefed up' compared with other recent bulkers, in effect taking account of what happened to the *Derbyshire* and to her sister ships, and to the hundreds of lost bulkers worldwide. Lloyd's Register is in the process of adjusting its practices, tightening up on stress analysis; insurers will inspect their clients' ships more thoroughly, load lines may well be adjusted for older bulk carriers. The arguments are won. So where is the need for a fuss? Where, in the British way of sweeping the awkward parts under the carpet, while conceding the substantive matter, is there any need to continue?

When Tim Madge asked some of the *Derbyshire* widows at the Mission to Seamen in Liverpool why, after all this time, they kept up their efforts to get to the bottom of what had really happened on that stormy day in 1980, they each answered in their own way. Substantially, however, they said the same: with no menfolk to bury, it was a prime necessity to believe that the truth, all the truth, had been made public.

To begin to understand their attitude after all this time, we must look at them as people, not statistics, and at how their lives were changed, if not ruined, by this single tragedy.

3

Decline and Fall: British shipping 1970–1990

The past twenty years have been the most critical for British shipping since the days of Drake and Raleigh. The events which have led to what many see as the catastrophic decline of the British registered merchant fleet have been largely unremarked by people outside the industry.

To seafarers though, this decline, and the feeling that no one really cares, have been a deeply wounding experience, made worse by their belief that Britain is still utterly dependent on sea-borne goods for her trade. Bringing goods in and out in British ships is not only the way to keep prices down, they say. It helps the balance of payments. Yet by 1989 only 21 per cent of imports and exports by weight, 35 per cent by value, were shipped in British registered vessels.

One seed of the current situation was sown in the 1960s, when a Labour government encouraged investment in new ships through a grant scheme designed to aid ailing British shipyards. Then came the oil crisis of 1973; oil prices, which *quadrupled* that year, doubled again by 1978.

By an irony, this was the time the British registered fleet had reached its zenith in tonnage terms; all too much, for the trade to sustain it was no longer there, affected by many factors and damaged most by those oil price rises. There was, too, pressure on the cross-trades through a United Nations Conference on Trade and Development (UNCTAD) of 1974, whose results were designed to help developing countries. But that huge tonnage reflected as well on the use of the British flag of convenience by foreign owners. It was not a false dawn; in fact it was the last rays of sunset.

From the pinnacle of tonnage (around 33 million gross registered tonnage[1] in 1975), the British registered fleet fell away, particularly in the post-Falklands War period, until by 1988 it had reached the lowest registered tonnage since 1900 (about 8 million grt). There was serious talk of there being no deep-sea merchant fleet by 1999.

Because what happened revolves around the issue of fleet registration, we need to examine, briefly, why so much energy was directed by the growing lobbies for government and public action on British shipping at this one issue: the British register.

All ships have to find a home. But because shipping has been an international business for so long, where a ship might 'flag' can be a complex question for an owner to answer. The truth is that for some years the cost of registration has been the critical issue, rather than any sentiment or, as in the past, the question of nationality.

The British register is now very expensive,[2] not from joining alone but in following the subsequent procedures by which a ship is accepted as complying with British shipping and safety legislation. Precisely because British shipping has had such a good safety record, the inspection of equipment is much more thorough than would be the case for many other registers; and the manning requirements, even the paperwork, all have financial implications. Further – and this raises the price no end – a British registered ship has to have British officers on the bridge and in the engine room. Then, vitally, there is the question of taxation.

In the past (and we might date this backwards from 1970) one of the main reasons for keeping a British ship registered here was the sense of national pride. Flying the red ensign was not unlike flying the white. Furthermore it attracted shippers who knew that their goods would be safe in British ships.

More commercially-minded American shipowners had long before moved away from the Stars and Stripes and into Panama, Honduras or Liberia. These principal flags of convenience (Focs) provide a very cheap registration with very liberal laws. (One had only to think of the state of Liberia, locked in a furious civil war in 1991, to recognise that its ships were not going to be inspected at all in the near future.)

Furthermore local taxation for registered shipping in these countries, if it exists, tends to be nominal. But it has to be said that while Britain enjoyed its golden period in shipping, and when our taxes were low, a hundred years or so ago, we effectively operated a flag of convenience, backed, however, by a powerful navy. This happened again, because of a change in the law, in the 1970s when foreign owners flocked to the British flag. The shipbuilding incentive schemes of the late sixties meant foreign owners came back; hence in the early 1970s Britain briefly enjoyed the status once again of a flag of convenience.

The answer to the question, 'How big is the British merchant fleet?' is not as easy as it seems. But the flight from the mainland register has been startling. To understand what happened, and why there are legitimate worries, we must look at the container revolution.

The idea is simple: instead of loading a ship with thousands of bits of cargo, as used to happen in the old 'break-bulk' ships, you 'stuff' a box of an agreed size, anywhere on land convenient to you. You then arrange its trans-shipment to the docks where a specialised crane drops it on the deck or in a space in the hold of a ship, alongside hundreds of other boxes of exactly the same size.

Dropped off at its destination, the box is then taken away to be unloaded where the recipient desires. Of course, each of these boxes may be sub-divided into dozens of compartments for the benefit of importers and exporters, each of whom has only a tiny quantity of material to ship; it all reduces shipping costs. How that is dealt with is no longer the problem of the shipping company.

The result is an economist's dream: ships which might have spent days, even weeks in a port loading and unloading can now turn round in a matter of hours. Even better, dockers are more or less eliminated; the ship's own deckhand complement can be drastically cut. Knowledge of how to operate deck cranes and winches, how to seal holds with tarpaulin and wood wedges, is no longer needed.

To give an idea of what the 'revolution' was about, see the following list and its instructions.

Commodity	No/Ton Wt	S/F	Remarks
Antimony	20 bags	30	Poisonous – keep clear of food
Beans	11 large 22 small	65/70	Generally clean but inspect for beetle . . .
Bitumen	6 drums	60	Stow on end and spread sand on decks underneath
Lime	casks/bags	60	Dry stow
Linseed	12 bags	60	Clean dry stow. Liable to heat, so keep well ventilated

The extracts are from a booklet[3] which lists around 250 different cargoes likely to be loaded or unloaded in East African ports. It gives the number (of bags/bales, etc.) per ton, the stowage factor (the amount of cubic feet likely to be taken up per ton) – and then lists the problems associated with the particular cargo.

Mates loading a mixed cargo had more to think about than how much space it would take. Put tea next to almost anything with an odour and it is spoilt; put explosives next to corrosives and the whole ship might go up. Other cargoes were liable to be riddled with insects, to sweat, leak, to catch fire when packed tight wet, or to poison anyone who injudiciously inspected it when stowed.

Often stowage was so complicated that a 'supercargo', a man not a package, had to be carried on voyages purely in the role of stowage expert. A whole book – Thomas's *Stowage*[4] – was compulsory reading for mates tramping general cargo ships round the world.

Ships would load these mixed cargoes, stuffed to their gunwales (so tight, one ex-mariner said, that you could not get a pin between bales), 10,000 tons or more, in five or six ports around the UK or Europe. They would sail for the Far East, whence they would unload in half a dozen ports, often coming alongside, often lying at anchor and unloading into lighters, in some of the most romantic rivers in the world. This was the 'pull' for all those old, deep-sea sailors, if no other.

These ships carried a complex knitting-needle-and-wool pattern of derricks on deck for self-loading and unloading. It all took time – and manpower. In the rest of the world manpower came cheap. In Britain the dockers were highly organised and very much in charge of what got loaded and unloaded, when, and for how much.

The container cut a swathe through most of this and although general cargo break-bulkers may still be found in small or far-flung ports, increasingly even the ships that undertake this form of coasting now carry containers. The major trade routes, all the big ports, are containerised.

By 1965 the first container consortium had been formed by P and O, Blue Funnel, British Commonwealth and Furness Withy. Others followed; but the change to containerisation was so expensive even large shipping companies balked at going it alone.

The new container ships were custom built. That was only the start. New port facilities had to be built, new depots for the containers across entire countries, new lorries had to be ordered to distribute the boxes, as did new railway trucks. The boxes had to be made, along with tanks, contained in box-size frames; millions of them. Computers were needed to keep track of them all, so shortages in boxes in any part of the world might not occur.

This was the world's first integrated transport system, eventually to operate in every country. It is fair to say it has transformed people's thinking about cargo handling and carrying; the start-up costs, overall, were staggering but the long-term savings have been greater.

The first purpose-built ship, the *Encounter Bay*, made her maiden run in March 1969 from Europe to Australia, which was fitting since it had been an Australian run from Melbourne to Fremantle five years before that had operated the first 'cellular' container ship.

The alterations in ship design were even more revolutionary than the changes in cargo handling. The ships were faster in turn-round but also much bigger. Estimates vary but today a single container ship is probably equivalent to ten or twelve old cargo vessels. If nothing else, these ships were going to ensure a huge reduction in the number of cargo ships operating around the world.

It was a part of the growing competitiveness of world shipping. In economic terms shipping is a near 'perfect' market, a classic of economic theory. But, like all theories, the perfection is marred by the constant interference of myriad factors.

In cargo carriage in the liner trade – the regular runs between ports – the British had set up a cartel system of liner 'conferences', which allowed some shipping companies in, kept others out, set rates and apportioned business. The same system was set up in passenger trades. Some conferences were open and any carrier could join. Others were strictly controlled. The same system operates in airlines today and is much reviled as a means of keeping prices high. In shipping the evidence is that conferences did not, on the whole, damage trade; prices stayed low. What the old-style conference probably did, however, was to keep British shipping too complacent for too long. And as so many conferences were dominated by the British, their demise was bound to affect British shipping more than others.

Conferences did not apply to tramping, of course. But tramping, the old stalwart trade for many British shipping companies, was going through its own convulsions. Two of these can be isolated: the development of bulk carriers; and the United Nations Conference on Trade and Development of 1974. As a direct result of this conference, developing countries were to secure a 40 per cent share of their own liner trade; 40 per cent was reserved to the country to which goods were sent or whence they came. Only 20 per cent was reserved to cross-traders. In many cases these had been exclusively British shipping firms.

The container ship development paralleled the change from the old tramps to bulkers and OBO carriers. These ships were huge by comparison with trampships. They could be built thanks to advances in technology, and because, after a certain size (65,000 dwt), there was no rise in crew costs. The size of all cargo ships had been growing steadily. But it was in oil tankers that the first true giants emerged. Oil, the fuel on which all the world's ships were running by the 1970s, was to create the biggest upheaval of all; both its extraction and its carriage affected British shipping profoundly.

British shipping, which invented the first oil tanker, the *Gluckauf*, in 1888, turned its back on the tramping side of this trade until almost too late. The big oil companies owned their own fleets; as for the rest – that is, charter carriage – it was dominated by private owners such as the Greeks Onassis and Niarchos.

In 1956 when the Suez Canal was closed for a few months oil tankers had to come out of the Persian Gulf and sail the longer Cape of Good Hope route. As a result they grew much larger. So large, in fact, that, along with the huge bulk carriers emerging in the late 1960s, they became known as 'Capesizers', ships big enough to justify the extra distance they had to travel around Africa. The extra time it took to sail them from one deep-water anchorage to another was offset by their immense cargo. More and more oil was required by the world's industries – and its cars. This unstoppable demand however was brought to a standstill, temporarily, in 1973 when the Arab States went to war and the consequent rise in the price of oil affected shipping worldwide. There followed a ten-year slump, compounded by an already ruinous over-ordering worldwide of new tonnage, much of it for giant oil tankers. By the late 1970s the very largest of these (for example the *Batillus* owned by Shell) could lift 550,000 dwt of oil.

In Britain, from 1964 a Labour government scheme allowed a 20 per cent subsidy for any new ship ordered, which was increased in 1967 to 25 per cent. The ship had to be on the British register for five years, but, bizarrely, could be built anywhere in the world. Nearly a thousand ships were built and as a result many foreign companies set up in the UK. In the mid-1970s these ships were still appearing, adding to the over-tonnage the oil crisis had created.

For British seafarers the slump was made worse because it followed after an unprecedented demand for their services by shipping companies desperate for trained men. It was all, so soon, to end. The end of passenger liners, the demise of the old, heavily manned break-bulkers, the cost of employing seamen, all contributed to a fall in the number employed.

World merchant tonnage had doubled in the twenty years from 1945 to 1965; and by 1975 it had doubled again, including between 1968 and 1972 an average of 30 million tons of new ships ordered; and in 1973 alone, just before the oil crisis, 70 million extra tons. Bankers, convinced that oil demand was unstoppable, lent huge sums of money to owners. Because ships take time to build, world tonnage peaked in 1982 at 425 million grt. By then trade was shrinking fast; there was a huge over-tonnage and a huge over-capacity among the world's shipbuilders; and in 1988 when British Shipbuilders (nationalised in 1977) employed a mere seven thousand men the subsidies were so large just to keep the whole mess going that it would have been cheaper to pay each man £30,000 a year to stay at home.

British shipping was affected in other ways. Oil price rises had stimulated a crash programme in marine engine research, which was to mean by the late 1980s that marine diesels could be run on what had previously been thought of as oil sludge, at far greater economy. The oil crisis stimulated the North Sea oil explorations; the British government was determined to wean us from Arab oil. In this they were not unsuccessful – North Sea oil is not the same kind; actually it is better. By 1990 Britain had become the world's fifth largest oil exporter and our domestic economy had been saved from imminent disaster. It meant a whole new shipping business in support vessels (rising from under 100 in 1973 to nearly 300 in 1986); but it also meant our outlook was shortened even more, back to our own shores. Far more important, our joining the Common Market meant that by the 1980s we had 60 per cent of our trade with countries just across the Channel and the North Sea. The one sector of British shipping which has continued to expand has been the short-sea ferry business.

It is worth noting that although most goods have to arrive and leave across the sea, 25 per cent of goods from Japan to Europe travels not by ocean-going ship but across the Russian railway system. Thereafter ferries may be involved – but not for much longer. Meanwhile Rotterdam and its huge Europort considers itself a major British port.

These changes – oil prices, North Sea oil and gas, containerisation, Europe, the loss of liner and cross-trades, protectionism and nationalism abroad – have all happened very suddenly to an industry which, while dealing in short-term forecasts, builds ships in the (economically) long-term.

To sum up, in 1970 British shipping was buoyant and expanding, having pioneered the great container revolution. By the mid-1980s it was in the middle of a massive slump. None of this was helped by the Conservative governments between 1979 and 1990.

*   *   *

One of the arguments used by anyone connected with the sea to explain why governments have tended to be largely indifferent to the plight of shipping in recent years is that 'the sea has no constituency'. Apart from that there is a long-held view that shipowners do very well for themselves. In the past this was probably true; the old shipping patriarchs — Vesteys, Inchcapes, Cunards, Harrisons, Bibbys, Ellermans and so on — ended up millionaires, their families inheriting great wealth.

Today shipping is a business like any other, except that returns on investment tend to be lower and the risks higher. There lies the problem; for a sensible company with a chance of investing money outside shipping as a fence against loss would, inevitably, begin to move away from ships and anything to do with them.

Shipping is absolutely dependent on the level of world trade. To paraphrase a saying: if the world economy catches a cold, shipping gets pneumonia. Government policies between 1979 and 1983 depressed the domestic British economy, sending it into the worst slump it had known for fifty years. This great shake-out affected shipbuilding — and therefore British shipping. It also meant there could be no help in any form for the merchant navy, whatever happened. Because of a historical accident (the Falklands war) and the vital part played by the merchant navy, many people thought the government would act neutrally in any future dealings. Sadly, that was not to be.

The Falklands War meant a task force. For the public the revelation came when it was seen that a naval task force needed an immense fleet train to sustain it, let alone troop carriers and hospital ships. In all fifty-one merchant ships were requisitioned. A new word entered the English language, alongside 'yomping': STUFT — ships taken up from trade. Among the oldest and most loved of ships, the *Uganda*, which became a hospital ship, and then a ferry for Argentine prisoners back to the mainland, was taken from a school cruise.

For landlubbers in the UK the whole armada just seemed to grow endlessly. For defence planners, this was what they had worked towards. In 1982 it was already getting hard to find the range of ships needed for an operation like the Falklands campaign. By 1991 and the Gulf War, almost no British-registered ships could be found to transport military supplies. It became apparent then, by the end of 1982, that we might have seen the last time when a Royal Navy task force could be fully supported by an all-British registered fleet train.

After the victory, the single change which ensured that the British-owned merchant fleet would flee the British register was not a concern by shipowners that their fleet might be taken up from trade again. It was the 1984 Finance Act, which cleaned up Corporation Tax.

What happened was this. From the early 1950s new British ships were supported by investment allowances, to begin with at a rate of 20 per cent, then from 1957 at 40 per cent. There were also means by which deprecia-tion costs on ships could be offset against profits (and therefore tax). In 1966, as we have seen, all this changed when the government introduced investment grants of 20 per cent. By 1971 under the Conservative govern-ment of Mr Heath, there had been a run-down of the grant scheme; its benefits to shipping continued because of the time-lag between ordering and launching ships. There was still 100 per cent depreciation though, on the first year's operation, and a 'carry-back' against the profits of the three years before that.

In evidence to the House of Commons Select Committee on Transport in 1986, the General Council of British Shipping pointed out that these latter allowances were: 'a major help to British shipowners. They allowed full write-off of the cost of buying a ship against profits virtually whenever they occurred. By the use of leasing arrangements with banks and other institutions they effectively injected fresh capital into the industry.'[5] The Report added that in this way British shipping was subsidised as other (foreign) shipping industries were. The 'table was level'.

All these allowances ended with the Budget of 1984. The result was a catastrophic flight from the British shipping register.

Sympathy for the shipowner was muted, and with good cause because, as we shall see, although the British registered fleet was to fall for the next six years, to reach its lowest recorded level this century by 1990, the flight was from the register not from shipping.

British shipping in 1990 was in no bad shape at all; indeed its prospects were beginning to look very good indeed as the world came out of the trade slump. Apart from that, shipbuilding may well pick up as huge tonnages of new ships are needed in the next ten years.

After decades of peace, the Falklands War had thrown into sharp relief the strategic value of Britain's merchant navy.

Ever since the Second World War and the menace of enemy U-boats, naval planning had determined that the Royal Navy would concentrate on anti-submarine warfare in the North Atlantic. This would ensure that the convoys of ships bringing supplies to Europe would not be sunk by Soviet submarines. But it had become clear that the convoys of ships crossing between Europe and the USA would be vital to reinforce NATO, should the Soviets attack. In that respect a large-scale European war was envisaged as being *exactly* like the Second World War.

STUFT was 'invented' with arcane debates about how many ships would be needed to make the system work. In the 1980s this debate became public; as well, it got mixed up with the 'short, fat' versus the 'long, thin' warship argument, along with other arguments about Soviet intentions. Suffice it to say here that the reduction in the British shipping register was used to beat government with the big stick of 'too few ships'.

For years British seafarers had felt marginalised by British society. They might be the means by which 98 per cent (today 95 per cent) of imports and exports came and went; nobody appeared to know or care. Then, at a time when huge structural changes had been taking place, they found they had a public issue, based on their heroic actions in the South Atlantic.

What followed was a heated argument increasingly confused by statistics. Part of the problem was that the meaning of different figures was different, for example: gross registered tonnage is a measure of *volume*; deadweight tonnage is used for merchant ships, displacement tonnage for warships.[6] The biggest change in usage has come about since the demise of the old cargo ships. The older method of measurement in gross registered tons has been replaced by deadweight figures (which give the lifting capacity of a ship), a more accurate way of assessing things.

Underlying all this was the defence argument: the die-hards took the old view that if a ship was not on the British register in time of national emergency its British owners could not be relied upon to bring it into the fold for requisition. This argument could not address the tricky question of a foreign-owned ship on the British register. If the crew was not largely British, or British colony, then it would be an equally shaky proposition. Thus was the circle complete: Britain needed a vastly enlarged merchant fleet, it needed to reverse the trend which had closed down Merchant Navy colleges, and it had to keep the Royal Navy at a level set more or less by the size of the fleet in 1980.

At the end of 1988 the major lobbies – the General Council of British Shipping and the British Maritime Charitable Foundation, along with the Marine Society, NUMAST, the officers' union, and the NUS, the seamen's union – all concluded that the end was in sight. Two hundred years after the loss of the American colonies, the single event which precipitated so much of our subsequent mercantile and naval history, what were the facts?

The area where most concern about British registered merchant ships was felt was in the deep-sea fleet – the field where traditionally we were strongest. In 1979 the British registered fleet was fourth in the world – ahead of the USSR, Norway, and even Panama. In 1983 the tonnage had fallen by nearly a third (in gross tonnage terms). By 1988 the total fleet had dropped by a further 60 per cent; we had fallen from fourth place in the world to eleventh in under ten years. In deadweight terms the fleet had fallen by about the same amount: (60 per cent) between 1983 and 1987, a two-fifths drop in the the number of ships, by early 1987 the deep-sea fleet numbered 193 vessels (a 60 per cent drop from 1983 when it consisted of 461 vessels). Most startling, there had been a drop of 80 per cent in numbers since 1978 (when there were 955 registered). This was the greatest reduction in fleet size for any maritime nation. But it could reasonably be argued that it reflected the sophistication of the British shipping industry, not its demise as was once thought. Precisely because British shipping was the most internationalised, it had little interest in sentiment or base nationalism. When circumstances dictated, the flag would be transferred elsewhere.

Even so, for anyone watching on the fringes, the results were spectacular and could easily be read to imply that Britain was determined to get right out of the market. Between 1983 and 1987 there were 204 direct sales of ships out and only thirty additions bought in; ninety-three vessels were flagged out (treble the rate of the previous five years).

The British container fleet declined by a third (to fifty-seven vessels) – but, please note, this meant only a drop of one-sixth in carrying capacity. Larger container ships were now arriving on the scene. The refrigerated ships (reefers) reduced by 75 per cent, leaving only six. Of those lost, sixteen were sold, nine flagged out – virtually all because crew costs were too high.

In bulk carriage, the British fleet fell by 60 per cent (most of the rest of the OECD countries, excluding Japan and Greece, experienced a 50 per cent drop). The British bulk fleet in 1987 consisted of forty-one vessels; only six 'true' British owners were left. Over-tonnage was the main reason for the drop.

The tanker fleet fell by 70 per cent, leaving seventy-six vessels, half of which belonged to the oil majors. Many tankers were shifted to Foc registers. British Petroleum flagged out to Bermuda. Again, over-tonnage was the main reason for the changes.

Passenger and cruise ships increased by one (to only seven vessels though) but Cunard had flagged out five ships.

Only in the short-sea trades had there been significant new investment. The British Maritime Charitable Foundation, perhaps the most vociferous lobbyist for British shipping during this time, commissioned a report on this decline (many of whose figures I have used above).[7] They concluded that:

Poor market and financial pressures have continued to be the dominant reasons for decline. High operating costs, particularly crew costs, have featured more strongly as a reason for sale or flagging out . . . The major changes to the UK shipping environment . . . have been the reduction in fiscal allowances for ships, the increased differential on crew costs relative to other flags and a relatively more depressed market *on which this differential matters* [our emphasis].

The report felt that flagging out had become the only way, in a depressed yet still competitive market (in numbers of suppliers) where marginal costs had become so critical, that owners could survive.

The period up to 1988 saw substantial changes in British shipping companies: more consortia appeared, companies diversified or simply got out of the market altogether. The oil companies cut back their own fleets. Foreign shipowners had more or less deserted the British register.

Put another way, the British share of world deadweight tonnage had now fallen from 20 per cent in the 1940s and 1950s; 12 per cent in the 1960s; 10 per cent in the mid-1970s to around 4 per cent in 1983. In 1987 it was reduced to under 2 per cent.

In all 268 deep-sea vessels had disappeared from the British register between 1983 and 1987. Even by the late 1980s there was little sign of new investment; the British fleet was now ageing as well as getting smaller. Predictions about its demise by 1999 now looked optimistic. Some commentators began to link the disappearance of the deep-sea fleet with the opening date for the Channel Tunnel.

4

A Family Tragedy

Forty-four people died on the *Derbyshire*; of those forty-two were the crew, officers and ratings. Two were wives. The practice of allowing wives to voyage with their husbands has become a normal part of shipping operations. In the case of the *Derbyshire* it adds a further dimension to the disaster. For disaster it was. One of the most shocking things the grieving widows and parents, sons, daughters and friends had to cope with was their prior belief that the *Derbyshire* was invincible. So many of those we have talked to still harp back to that one point: how could she have sunk, she was so large? In a very straightforward way, then, the *Derbyshire* can be directly likened to the *Titanic*, that previous symbol of unsinkability.

Grief follows a pattern; in time wounds heal. But that depends on a process, a vital part of which is being able to say goodbye to the dead, to bury them. Anger, guilt, sorrow all play a part in this natural process and, however violent the end of a loved one, a means to come to terms with what happened is eventually found. To an outsider the impact of grief on the faces of the families of the *Derbyshire* crew is palpable, etched-in permanently. They still cry after all these years, easily and without shame, at the memories. But what becomes immediately apparent is that their grief is not only for the dead they could not bury but also for what happened afterwards; for the years of struggling to have the questions surrounding the *Derbyshire's* death resolved, for what they heard at the formal inquiry; they shed tears of despair that they will never escape this horror.

Most touching of all, they grieve for the ship, a deep, heartfelt sorrow that something of such grace and power could be lost in this way. The *Derbyshire* was a bulk carrier, a humble worker, but to those who remember her, still a kind of miracle in her sheer enormity. It is hard to imagine a ship the width of a six-lane motorway, a steel structure a fifth of a mile long, moving through the water. In a world grown used to big things, she was among the very biggest.

On a tiny scale compared with this ship is the house set back a little way on the edge of Corby, where Marion Baylis lives. It is close to the railway station, now abandoned, like her life. She is the widow of the Chief Officer, 'Curly' Baylis. His portrait still grins at her from a framed photograph on the bookcase. Marion spent years in limbo after his death. But she and Curly had three children – Pam, seventeen; Richard, sixteen; and Simon, fourteen. Their individual reactions were something more for her to bear:

> Richard had to shut it out – it wasn't happening. John Craven's *News-round* did a piece on the television. They obviously said it so simply for the children. My sister-in-law and myself and the three children were watching. Pam cried, Simon cried – I cried – but Richard just sat there and said, 'I don't know what the fuss is all about.'

A few days later Richard was at school when a friend told him, 'They've called the search off.' Marion remembers:

> The poor lad walked all the way home from school and told me. I rang Bibby Line and a voice said, 'Because of bad weather in the area the search has been called off. When the weather improves the search will be resumed – but not to look for survivors, just for wreckage.' I said, 'Oh, so I must presume death?' and the voice said, 'Yes.' I said, 'Thank you very much,' and put the phone down. With hindsight I am now furious and angry about the way that was done but at the time I didn't react at all. I came back into this room and I couldn't use the word 'dead' – I still find it difficult. I said, 'Dad's not coming home'. That was it. I went round to my parents-in-law and told them. I think they talked about a shopping trip. I thought, 'I can't cope with this, I am going to have hysterics,' so I left them and went to my own father and said, 'Curly's not coming home, Dad.' Then I came home to this house. That was eleven years ago.
>
> You have caught me at a bad time because my father died this August [1991] and it has dredged up so much. I am sure I am not going mad but it sometimes feels like it. Part of me *is* grieving but I can't work it out. I have had to accept it here, in my head. I have had to keep going. I have had to go shopping, all the daily things. It sapped my confidence so much, I don't know how I managed. And anybody who visited me in those first days was brave – very, very brave. A lady visited me who had lost her husband and while she was talking I could feel the words rising up inside me, wanting to say, 'You're lucky you had a body, you're lucky.' I kept on thinking all these nasty things I wanted to shout at her. Then, a fortnight after, I put my smile on. Everyone said, 'You'll be OK, once the funeral's over.' We never had that. The memorial service was not the same. I used to pace the house and I'd think, 'If only I could talk

to someone, I'd give anything to be able to say what I felt to someone else who knows what I am going through.' I hadn't the courage to phone up Bibby Line and ask them, 'Can I talk to another family, please, there must be a family, a widow to whom I can talk without having to explain, without having to pretend.' I never did. Then a friend said, 'Listen to Radio Four tonight' – this must have been about 1986 – 'there's a programme about the *Derbyshire*.' That's when I found out about the *Derbyshire* Families Association.

Marion subsequently became Secretary of the Association, a move which probably saved her sanity. But the years have taken their toll, she believes, in particular of her physical health. As she puts it, 'The pain of the bereavement has destroyed so much.'

At the same time she found new strength. One turning point, where her anger became focused, was the formal inquiry, which she attended nearly every day from October 1987 to March 1988. 'I met many other people there, other families, but mostly I got so incensed at the attitude of the legal teams. They laughed, they joked. I know their attitude is that you must not get involved, but it jarred.' She had to sit, day after day, week after week, suppressing her own feelings. Only towards the end, in the last week, when it was suggested that the *Derbyshire* had never previously been in bad weather, she burst out: 'Rubbish!'

Marion knew it was untrue: Curly had written to tell her of a liferaft wrenched from its mountings.

In his own inimitable style he had written, 'We've been playing sailors with oilskins.' So I knew there had been bad weather. But what a nonsense to suggest she had never previously been in bad weather. And the idea that the first time she met some she would sink . . . In any case a smaller ship came through that storm.

A bigger shock for Marion Baylis had come the year before the formal inquiry, when she first heard that the *Derbyshire* might have sunk because of massive structural failure. Not knowing how a ship of her size could be overwhelmed in a storm, she had nevertheless found that easier to accept than what she knows now:

Having to cope with my three children, it was easier for me to say it was the weather, even though I thought at the back of my mind, 'How could it affect a great big ship like that?' because I knew the size of it. I was so angry then, and that anger has never left me. I picked up my pencil and I have never stopped writing since. That, and the inquiry – which also made me wild. They can't wait for us all to die. Our children, our grandchildren will carry this on. People have said to me, 'Well, it was their job,' implying, I suppose, that we should all shut up and stop moaning. I want to know, I want to see it in black and white that these ships are being built properly. Otherwise Curly's death has been absolutely useless.

Dave Ramwell first met Cathie Musa, widow of Ronnie, an able seaman on the *Derbyshire*, in 1989 after the memorial service in Liverpool Cathedral:

A small convoy of vehicles threaded its way from the Anglican cathedral to a small school nearby. Those good people who all of us – to our shame – tend to take for granted appeared among us in the school hall with tea and cakes. The air buzzed with subdued conversation, thickened with cigarette smoke. Vikki King, chairperson of the MV *Derbyshire* Families Association spoke. She was able to tell everyone how in her recent visit to Sept Iles (in Canada, where the *Derbyshire* left on her last voyage), the Seamen's Mission padre had assured her and her husband, Des, that the atmosphere on the ship had been contented and happy when she sailed.

I was never so aware of invading private grief as at that meeting. Eyes were watering freely. I wanted to tell everyone about an article I wrote in *Sea Breezes*[1] but I felt it was too presumptuous. I did manage a brief talk with Cathie Musa and, yes, she said, she would like me to help, she would like *anyone* to help. She had come to terms with her grief, sadness was still in her tears though. But more than that there was now anger and frustration.

Cathie, a Glasgow lass, fell in love with Ronnie Musa and has never lost that first wild flush of true romance. Worn down by grief and poverty, when she remembers him her eyes are still alight. With Cathie the depth of this tragedy is shown by the gap between her natural toughness and her stricken incoherence, after all this time, when she talks of Ronnie. Her grief is large, it involves all the crew: tears spring easily when she talks of 'those young boys' she saw at the airport that last time, on their way to join the ship in France.

When the initial shock had worn off Cathie went to Bibbys, to enquire about the lifeboat that had been found:

I was shown into Mr Bibby's office; I never saw the old man, I saw his son. I asked him about the lifeboat and he told me they weren't even sure if it was theirs. He asked another man who was there to go to the safe and to bring the photo. When I looked it was such a small object in a big sea . . .

Cathie believed – wanted so badly to believe – that if one lifeboat had been found perhaps the other one had got away from the stricken ship, and, if so, its crew could either still be in the area, drifting, or had made it to an island. Her hopes were systematically dashed. Like Marion Baylis, it was only in 1986 that she discovered there could be another reason why the ship had sunk: 'Until then I still would not believe my Ronnie was gone. I kept thinking that one day he would knock on the door. Then I was shown a much larger picture of that lifeboat and it shattered my dreams and my hopes and my life.'

It is with the widows of the men lost on the *Derbyshire* that one comes closest to the heart of this matter, in human terms. All lives are lost one day, so to speak, and seafaring is still a hazardous trade. It wrenches apart ordinary lives by its nature: long absences are the norm. But wives get used to that and their marriages are frequently much stronger than the average. Certainly an understanding of what takes their menfolk off on long voyages, and thus a close psychological appreciation of that great, enduring mistress, the sea, makes these women remarkable. There is a great divide, in seafaring, between short-sea trading and 'deep sea', the latter retaining all the grandeur and mystery that Joseph Conrad wrote about.

Jim Noblett, husband of Margaret, and an able seaman on the *Derbyshire*, had tried short-sea trades. But his sea was the Irish, out of Liverpool, and one of the most treacherous in the world:

One particular voyage he did, he came back early in the evening, I was in bed, and he was absolutely devastated. 'Margaret,' he said, 'I have never been as frightened in all my life.' It had been a containership, loaded with farming machinery, like combine harvesters, on deck and it had been such a bad storm that they had lost everything off the deck. He wasn't a religious man but he told me he had prayed. You know, he actually cried when he remembered how bad it had been and he was a big man, six foot, and he had been at sea since he was sixteen. He said then that when he could he would go for much bigger ships because, he said, he'd have a better chance.

The biggest ships, of course, were and are the ocean-going containerships and bulkers. The voyage with the *Derbyshire* was Jim's fourth with Bibbys:

He was happy at sea. I used to say to him when he thought of coming ashore, 'Go on, get back, you've got to do what you're happiest doing.' You see, although they miss the children it was like being torn so there was no happy medium. When the children were little he used to say, 'Well, I will go on to deep sea; the ships are safer and the money is better.' That's what he used to say. He tried to come ashore when we were first married. He said, 'I'm going to try it for six months.' I think it was the worst six months of my life.

Even Ronnie Musa had tried to 'swallow the anchor' once. He and Cathie moved to London and he worked as a boilerman at the Maudsley Hospital in Denmark Hill. Every night he was home, but Cathie could see it was making his life a misery. She told him, 'Come on, I'm going back to Liverpool.'

When the *Derbyshire* was lost these women had no idea what was going to happen to them. In the event they all got a payment equivalent to a year of their husband's salary. What they all discovered, however, was that, in line with standard practice, their men were not insured for being at sea. As one of the women said, 'I got told that the seamen were insured for leaving the house to go to the ship – like when they were flown out to join. Once they boarded it stopped. The ship was insured but the men on board were not.'

Some widows found they could not get any state support because of their *ex gratia* payment. This meant they had to spend the money until it ran out. Another of the widows said, 'I couldn't go to the social because of that money. Finally they agreed to give me £22 a week, but when my pension came through they took that amount back off. I had to wait for that – £52 a week.'

The financial worries went along with the tribulations of the children:

My two youngest ones suffered the worst, a girl just turned fourteen, and a boy of eight. The little girl had just started her periods so she was having a hard time anyway. I'm talking straight now, I had three years of hell. For three years she was horrible to me, she wasn't my girl, not the one I knew. She's twenty-five now with a little baby of her own and she says, 'Mum, I was awful.' That was her way of handling it.

My little boy never spoke about it. It took him nine months and then I heard him crying in his bedroom; he broke his heart. I went in to him and he cried without stopping all night. I think, I really do, that if their dads had died here and they'd seen them dead, and then they had buried them and done their grieving, it would have been better. It was this aggro which just built and built.

Despite their fathers being away these children had adjusted. As Cathie used to say to neighbours commiserating over her husband's absences at sea:

> I said, 'I bet your husband isn't around half as much as mine. When mine is home he can be with the kids all the time, take and fetch them from school. Where does yours go of an evening? To the pub or club for a drink. My Ronnie doesn't drink, he goes into the kitchen. His one pleasure is to get a paper on a Saturday morning and then, Saturday afternoon, watch the racing on the telly.'

Emotional trauma and financial hardship faced the *Derbyshire* families, sometimes one more than the other. But, as we have tried to explain, one of the worst aspects of this story is that these families have never got over what happened. In this case what they suffer is close to a physical wound, a war wound.

It was not only the wives and children, of course; mothers and fathers lost sons; and two lost daughters. John and Sheila Jones read and re-read the letters and postcards from their son, David, the Second Engineer. They held out some hope in the immediate aftermath, as did Graeme Hutchinson's family in South Shields. Graeme had been the Third Engineer and, like David, had had his wife on board with him.

Peter Lambert, brother of Paul, was only eighteen when he died. He had, though, always known where he wanted to go. He had been about to marry his childhood sweetheart: 'This is going to be my last deep sea trip,' he told her, a prophetic and cruelly truthful remark. 'When I get back I'm going to look for a job on the dredgers.'

Charlie (no relative to Ronnie) Musa's mother had died a year before, in 1979. Now he had to face the prospect of bringing up his younger brothers and sisters. For widower Tom Chedotal, an ex-seafarer, he had to face the loss of his thirty-year-old son, Frederick, the ship's Electrical Officer.

'I knew in my heart that I'd never see my brother again,' said Harriet Ellison at her home in Hare Croft, Cantril Farm. And so it goes on: two of the crew, Mark Freeman, junior catering rating, and Adrian Stott, junior seaman, were too young to vote. Both came from inland towns, Mark from Oldham, Adrian from Macclesfield. Most of the other seamen came from around Liverpool, where seventeen families grieve in that ancient heart of British seafaring.

The initial impact of the sinking was over by the mid-eighties. There has since set in a double reaction. Some immersed themselves in the *Derbyshire* Families Association. Others, like Peter Ridyard, father of the Fourth Officer, David, set out to prove once and for all what actually happened. As a marine surveyor, he was well-placed among the relatives to undertake what became a long, hard job of detection spread over most of the globe.

A few, whose feelings must be respected, have wished their dead to rest in peace, not wanting even a ripple of pain to resurface.

We want to emphasise the human side of this story; to show that the lives lost in an event like this are as nothing to the damage that is done to a much broader group: the relatives first and foremost; but wider than that. Marion Baylis had no real help for years, no counselling, no proper support. It was an accident that she lighted upon the DFA. She remains bitter about those early years.

We have seen how the children were affected. Once, when communities of seafarers existed all round Britain, and sea disasters were more commonplace, we may surmise that sailors' relatives were helped by a community of interest and concern.

Part of the story is linked to Britain's abandonment of the sea. Her decline as a maritime nation has been evident for decades. It is particularly poignant that one of its more sharply downward phases should have occurred in the years after the *Derbyshire* sank. But the seeds were already there. British shipping has had a mixed history. Some parts have been glorious, others shameful. The treatment of sailors has, sadly, fallen for the most part into the latter category. Ships too: some have been built with pride, care and love; others rather hastily composed against fierce competition from abroad.

The Bridge class of OBOs were a product of one of the great changes in shipping. It was a double change – to containerships on the one hand, and to bulk carriers of increasing size on the other. The Bridge ships were a family, massive, complex. In the following chapter we find out how they came about and what happened to them.

5

The Bridge Class Ships: a family of woes

The *Derbyshire*, built between 1974 and 1976, was the last of the six Bridge class of OBOs to be built at the Haverton Hill shipyard of Swan Hunter. She was launched in January 1976. The six sister ships were:

BRIDGE CLASS	LAUNCHED
Furness Bridge	1971
afterwards *Marcona Pathfinder*	
Tyne Bridge	1972
afterwards *East Bridge*	
English Bridge	1973
afterwards *Kowloon Bridge*	
Sir John Hunter	1974
afterwards *Cast Kittiwake*	
Sir Alexander Glen	1975
Liverpool Bridge	1976
afterwards *Derbyshire*	

The *Derbyshire* was built under special survey to the full requirements of Lloyd's Register of Shipping, and was given the 100A1 classification. She was the length of three football pitches and, as we have said, the width of a motorway. With nine holds she had a capacity of over six million cubic feet. Her maximum deadweight (that is, the weight of cargo, fuel, water and stores) was about 166,000 tons, which gave her a draught of sixty feet in salt water. She could travel at 15 knots using about 95 tons of fuel oil a day. The single huge diesel engine, designed by the Danish company, Burmeister and Wain, and built under licence by Harland and Wolff of Belfast, was rated at 28,000 brake horsepower. The shaft turned at a mere 100 revolutions a minute at this output.

The OBO type first appeared in the mid-1960s. It offered great flexibility, being designed to carry cargoes of ore, bulk (such as grain) and oil. The ships were therefore very complicated in design, particularly because of the great differences between cargoes. They did not generally have longitudinal bulkheads and the main cargo compartments were used irrespective of the sort of cargo carried. In this sense, each hold might be likened to a giant box: there were no cross-girders within these holds in either direction and the strength depended on the integrity of the whole. The official inquiry report into the loss of the *Derbyshire*[1] says this of OBOs in general:

> Whilst the design of an OBO is more complicated than a tanker or bulk carrier or even an ore/oil ship, shipowners clearly believed that the potentially increased revenues from OBO ships would more than offset their increased cost. Hence the emergence of the OBO ship as a separate sector of the world shipping fleet.

The report goes on to enumerate the design philosophy. This includes a need:

> to provide full facilities for both dry and liquid cargoes . . . For example, both a bilge system and a cargo oil handling system had to be installed in association with wide hatches for grab handling of dry cargoes . . . Hatch covers had to provide watertight integrity of the main hull in addition to withstanding the sloshing loads from oil.

The structural problems were of a different order. The report says that there were known to be:

> high shear forces in the side shell structure caused by loading in alternate holds . . . Large hull girder bending moments . . . Extremely high bending and shear loads in *transverse* bulkheads [our emphasis], especially in way of the lower stools, because of the absence of horizontal stringers . . . torsion of the upper wing tank structure, particularly in ships with long holds, resulting in the buckling of web frames and the distortion of hatch openings.

Put more succinctly, these complicated ships suffered all kinds of problems from being too long and too open in design. The bigger ones, said the report, had bigger problems. Among the solutions were 'use of high tensile steels in the deck structure and double skin construction for the side shell and main transverse bulkheads'. But every 'solution' has a price: high tensile steels were light enough but they tempted builders to reduce the 'scantlings', that is, the overall dimensions of the ship per item: thinner girders, thinner plates, smaller brackets.

The Bridge class was designed towards the end of the 1960s when some of these problems were well known; others remained to be discovered. Incorporated in the design were double skin arrangements at the side shell (in fact wing tanks, see diagram) and double transverse bulkheads separating the holds. The overall design was for an OBO of around 150,000 tonnes deadweight (see Glossary) capable of carrying ore cargoes in alternate holds with appropriate, heavier scantlings; oil cargoes in all holds with surfaces pressed up to hatch coaming levels; bulk cargoes in all holds.

The concept was for a clean interior cargo hold surface to allow the free flow of ore, bulk or oil cargoes and fast easy cleaning of holds between successive voyages. There were, in each ship, nine cargo holds of equal length with hatches 14 square metres. These hatches were hydraulically operated, side-rolling, steel hatch covers divided down the centre line. They had to be both oil- and gas-tight.

The cargo holds had hopper-type bottoms at the sides and ends for easier unloading, and the upper surfaces were angled at 30° so that dry cargoes, like grain, completely filled the holds without the need for trimming. There were ballast tanks formed by the upper and lower wing tanks (see figures in Chapter 10). Double bottom tanks and wing tanks between the upper and lower hopper tanks were included.

Ship number 25 – the *Furness Bridge* when launched – and the first of the class, worked out at 926 feet long, 145 feet wide, drawing around 60 feet. She had a single diesel engine, at the time of fitting the highest-powered diesel engine built in Britain, providing a service speed of 15.5 knots. These ships were the first true OBOs built in the country and the largest bulk carriers British yards had ever turned out.

Given all these 'firsts' it is well worth looking at each ship in detail. We know what eventually happened to the *Derbyshire*. The *Kowloon Bridge* gets a chapter to herself (Chapter 8) as her history is so important to the overall story. What of the other four?

It is perhaps worth noting beforehand that all ships may be expected to have operational problems, caused perhaps by some elements of design or by unforeseen circumstances that occurred during building or launching, although these are not to be associated with any particular designer or builder. It is in the nature of shipping also to expect ships to suffer damage from time to time for a variety of reasons, whether they are poorly loaded or bad weather causes them to lose fittings or even to lose part of their cargo. Shipping is inherently a hazardous business. But we cannot stress strongly enough that these six ships were trailblazers built above the minimum criteria, huge vessels manned by highly-trained, European-based crews. Above all, they were *young* ships. All however had something else in common: in their operational lives they all suffered problems of cracking in and around Frame 65, the transverse bulkhead arrangement just ahead of the superstructure. Again it is worth stressing that this was the frame about which the official inquiry was eventually to decide that it was 'relatively stronger than the section at midships'; and to state that the building 'arrangements' did provide 'appropriate continuity of strength'.

Furness Bridge

We know that the first ship had a different arrangement as far as this frame was concerned. Yet the *Furness Bridge* required repairs at bulkhead 65 less than two years after she had been launched.[2] Eighteen months later cracks had occurred at frames 98, 133 and 193. Much more significant, in March 1982 (two years after the *Derbyshire* loss) she had reported cracked deck plating, which was renewed with higher grade steel; and an extensive crack in the vicinity of Frame 65.[3] What we do not know is whether increased vigilance had been suggested to the master of *Furness Bridge*, following the loss of the *Derbyshire* and the problems with the *Tyne Bridge*; but we suspect it had. For one of the problems with these cracks was finding them, unless they were so bad they started to appear on the deck.

Tyne Bridge

It was March 11th, 1982. On passage and in ballast from Hamburg, bound for Brazil, the *Tyne Bridge* encountered a North Sea storm. Suddenly, from somewhere just forward of the accommodation, the master heard the unmistakable sound of screeching metal. He sent one of his officers forward to investigate. The man reported that water was coming from the corner of number nine hold. The after bulkhead of this hold is Frame 65. There were, he said, cracks in the area.

Such was his concern that the master arranged for the majority of his crew to be air-lifted to safety. He then arranged a tow back to Hamburg. The ship was brought to the Blohm and Voss shipyard and repairs were begun under the supervision of the classification society, Registro Italiano Navale (the Italian equivalent of Lloyd's Register but acting on behalf of the Italian government as the vessel was registered in Italy). Lloyd's officials were present also.

The damage was severe. On the starboard side there was a 19-foot crack, on the port side an 11-foot crack. The Bishop, Price and Temarel paper, read to RINA, says this: 'Severe deck cracking in way of Frame 65. Crack propagation in deck probably associated with brittle fracture [see Chapter 9]. Portions of the deck plating cropped and renewed with higher grade plating.'

One of the keys to what happened here (and by simple logical extension, to the *Derbyshire*) is the relationship between the forward two-thirds of the ship and the last one-third (where the accommodation and superstructure are placed). We know that four of these ships had one port and one starboard underdeck longitudinal girder extending from bow to Frame 65 to give it longitudinal strength. At Frame 65 this was stopped at the forward side of the bulkhead. Crudely then, you have two structures welded at this point.

That was not the way the ships were designed; the *Furness Bridge* was built with longitudinals which penetrated beyond this frame, pinning the two parts of the ship together. But this arrangement was certainly changed in four of the other five ships, and we believe it was changed in the *Derbyshire* too.

The Lloyd's surveyor on the spot said, among other things, that in the *Tyne Bridge* all longitudinals connected to the bulkhead (mostly with pad) 'Would appear problems during building.'[4] However, it was ascertained by noting German lettering on the fitted pads that these must have been installed later at a German repair yard.

In the original design all longitudinals were carried through the bulkhead to maintain strength and hull integrity; in the *Tyne Bridge* this did not happen. The longitudinals were butted to each other on either side of the bulkhead. If these butted pieces are welded with the utmost care so that they are in perfect alignment, there is a form of structural continuity.

The Lloyd's man looking at the *Tyne Bridge* went on to say: 'Deck now cut away – misalignment of fore and aft structure *as expected*'[5] (our emphasis).

So crucial is this that we make no apology for returning to it time and again. To illustrate the problem, think of a table made of metal supported underneath by a girder-shaped piece of steel. If we place another steel girder on top, exactly in line with the girder underneath, nothing happens. If that top girder is misplaced by not very much, the table collapses. Try it with bricks and a piece of cardboard – but watch out for your toes.

Of course the girders were welded. But a ship is not a static object and the effects of movement, as encountered in the North Sea storm of March 1982, stressed the ship's hull beyond its limits. An Italian consulting company, brought in for the *Tyne Bridge* repairs, said in its report: 'The main cause of ruptures has to be attributed to the structural reasons.'[6] A later Department of Transport report added: 'An examination of the areas affected by the fractures had revealed the misalignment of longitudinal strength members. It was concluded that these would have led to possible stress concentrations.'[7] And in the same paragraph: 'Calculations showed significant stress concentrations where fractures had occurred . . . The suitability of the repair was confirmed by the substantially reduced stress concentration factors derived from calculation.'[8]

The report discusses the grades of steel used in the ship and says that they found that Grade A steel had been used. (Confusingly, Grade A steel is not as good as Grade D). It concludes:

Steel of Grade D would generally be required for the strength deck as follows–

a) where the thickness of the plate exceeds 20.5mm
    i) from *0.2 length* aft of amidships to length *0.2 forward of amidships*;
    ii) at the corners of openings and at breaks in the superstructures irrespective of position
b) in stringer plates outside of *0.4 length* amidships when the thickness exceeds 25.5mm (one inch).[9]

The rules about steel grades are decided by Lloyd's. In 1971 the Lloyd's Register Executive Board approved a change permitting the use of Grade A (i.e. inferior) steel in the places it was used in the *Tyne Bridge*.[10] The ships delivered after this date all had this lesser quality steel, including the *Derbyshire*. The deck plating and vital longitudinals in the vicinity of Frame 65 were composed of Grade A steel.

The *Tyne Bridge* left the German yard, her repairs complete, but she was not to survive much longer. (A ship of her type is normally reckoned to have a useful life of twenty to thirty years.) In 1989 she was sailed to Taiwan where she was scrapped, gone after just seventeen years.

Sir John Hunter

The *Sir John Hunter* was the fourth ship built. Before the *Tyne Bridge* incident, she had suffered cracks in the vicinity of Frame 65.[11] These had been repaired by gouging out the area and rewelding. By 1982 she was renamed the *Cast Kittiwake* and, shortly after the *Tyne Bridge* incident, was on her way to Wakayama in Japan, loaded with iron ore. Her owners, alerted by what had happened to *Tyne Bridge*, sent her master a warning.

When she was inspected at sea she was found to be suffering fractures 'in way of number nine after cargo hold'. On April 3rd and 4th, 1982, less than a month after *Tyne Bridge* cracked, she was inspected afloat by surveyors in Kashima, Japan. They found her longitudinals also terminated at bulkhead 65. Holes were drilled in this bulkhead to determine the extent of the misalignment. It was considerable. Once again, fitted pads had been installed on some previous occasion presumably due to defects arising in these areas; on the port side the plate was aft of it; on the starboard side, forward. Some temporary repairs were made.

As Kashima lacked the facilities to effect the extensive repairs required, the *Cast Kittiwake* continued to Wakayama. There she was given permission for one more commercial voyage, which ended in her being drydocked in Rotterdam in July 1982. According to one report: 'it was then found that the deck plating in way of the after corner of number nine hatch had developed cracks running diagonally aft and outwards . . . where longitudinal and transverse bulkheads meet at Frame 65 . . . cracked in way of welds and previous fitted doubler plates'.[12]

The report continued:

. . . when the deck plating was removed for renewal it was found numerous transverse floors and brackets where they should have been aligned on either side of the bulkhead were in fact misaligned by up to measured amounts of 50/55 mm (two inches). This could only have occurred at the building stages.[13]

Eventually repaired, *Cast Kittiwake* was cracking at bulkhead 65 by February 1984; wear and tear, it was said. In March 1987 there was 'rippling of the fore and aft bulkhead between the pumproom and the cofferdam from frames 63 to 65; other damage around Frame 65 was reported'.[14]

Sir Alexander Glen

The fifth ship, *Sir Alexander Glen*, had already reported a small fracture at Frame 65 (between number nine hold and the wing tanks) in September 1975, only months after launching. The problems associated with two of her sister ships in 1982 caused her to be issued with a warning while on passage, in her case from Hay Point, Australia to Taranto, Italy. Inspection by her crew revealed the bulkhead at Frame 65 to be 'fractured in several places on both port and starboard sides'. She continued to Italy where the cracks were 'veed out' and welded. However, by June 1982 new cracks were found in the same place and new repairs had to be made. In August 1982 severe cracking was found, again in Frame 65, but it did not extend to the main deck. A similar repair to that of the *Tyne Bridge* was then made.

Just over a year later, in October 1983 signs of stress were reported in a longitudinal bulkhead on the port side; and in February 1984 signs of excessive stress were found near Frame 65. Modifications made to her in Yokohama included the cropping and renewal of plating.

And so we come back to the *Derbyshire's* short life before she sank. She was named the *Liverpool Bridge* at her launching; and she and her sister *English Bridge* (later the *Kowloon Bridge*) were the biggest ships ever built for the old-established shipping firm, Bibbys, who have their offices in Liverpool. She was handed over to her owners, Bibby Tankers Ltd, in Hamburg on June 10th, 1976, at which point she was commissioned and then managed by Bibby Bros and Co. (Management) Ltd, another part of the Bibby Group, for the rest of her career.

Until 1977 Bibbys had chartered several of its ships to a consortium, Seabridge Shipping Ltd. This had been formed to serve the mutual interests of some leading British shipping lines who wished to trade in bulk cargoes. Ships managed by the consortium carried names ending in 'Bridge'. When at the end of 1977 Bibbys withdrew from Seabridge and managed their own ships, in keeping with the company's tradition of naming ships after English shires they changed the name of the *Liverpool Bridge* to the *Derbyshire*. *Liverpool Bridge* had already had an eventful life. Two days after she was commissioned, having sailed from Hamburg to Flushing in ballast, she was at anchor when an auxiliary boiler blew up, killing the Third Engineer and inflicting serious burns on the Electrical Officer, who died in hospital a few days later. The explosion caused considerable damage in the engine room where it had been powerful enough to bend a side frame and buckle rails and gratings. It broke cables and smashed pipelines and other fittings.

The full story of what happened was never established, partly because an electronic 'flame eye' went missing, part of the boiler control panel which was dumped in a shoreside skip after the accident. It would have helped the investigations but it had been removed, probably stolen, from the skip.

None the less the *Liverpool Bridge* left Flushing on July 5th, 1976 to load her first cargo, coal, from Hampton Roads in the USA. Thereafter she carried either iron ore, crude oil or coal, calling at ports worldwide in Brazil, Japan, Saudi Arabia, Iran, Canada, Indonesia, Australia and Finland.

There was one notable exception to the three 'standard' cargoes she carried. Crossing the Indian Ocean from Brazil, bound for Japan, Captain Underhill received a cable ordering his ship to Koh Sichang in Thailand, to load a cargo of bulk tapioca pellets for the Netherlands. The ship, by then the *Derbyshire*, arrived in January 1978. Captain Underhill wrote an amusing account of this operation in that year's spring issue of the Bibby Group house magazine, *The Bibby Gazette*. While he had not known exactly what to expect, he knew there would be an invasion: 'roughly 600 men, women and children poured on board and proceeded to turn the ship into a floating tent village.' A floating crane first placed lorry cranes on board, one on either side of each of the *Derbyshire*'s nine hatches. Tapioca, from barges lying alongside, was shovelled into nets and canvas bags and hoisted on to the partially opened hatch covers, where it was tipped into the holds, creating a cloud of tapioca dust so dense that the ship simply disappeared, looking forward from the bridge. Eventually the *Derbyshire*'s population swelled to 850 as restaurants, shops and casinos began to open on deck. Apparently the food to be had from the cafés was excellent, 'Sofias' being singled out for particular patronage by the crew. 'Charlies' was also much liked for its curries, although no one was quite sure what was being curried.

That expedition was a one-off for the *Derbyshire*. By 1978 a world slump in shipping was under way and after discharging her cargo in Europoort, Rotterdam she sailed to Stavanger, Norway where she was laid up for a year. Curly Baylis used to travel up from the UK from time to time, with a skeleton crew, to check that she remained in good condition.

She was finally reactivated in April 1979, sailing for Flushing on April 11th and thence to Sept Iles in Canada for the first of her cargoes of iron ore. Frame 65 problems had already started to occur. In November 1977, when eighteen months old, she had reported a fracture on the starboard side at the intersection of bulkhead 65 and the sloping bottom of the wing tank. This fracture was repaired in Daiwa in July 1979, that is, after her reactivation. And, as we have already mentioned, in April 1980 extensive cracking was again found at bulkhead 65, and was repaired this time in drydock at Sasebo, Japan.

So here we have six ships, built over a period of five years. By 1991 two had sunk, one had been scrapped. All six had suffered extensive and consistent problems in one place above all others: Frame 65, bulkhead 65, the point just ahead of the superstructure. The facts about the cracking in this area are incontrovertible and well attested by, among others, Lloyd's Register.

The *Derbyshire* sank, according to the official inquiry, due to bad weather.

Part II

A Deathly Silence

6

A Deepening Mystery

We now have a complex jigsaw puzzle before us and many of the pieces will be scattered for some time yet. We have seen one completed piece from this puzzle already – the larger section of the decline of British shipping. When an industry begins to go down, so do standards. And, as we have also seen, this has to be set against an aggressive government determined in the circumstances to 'liberate' industry from constraints. We argue that this inevitably includes constraints of safety.

The smaller section, and the one with which we are most concerned, is about the *Derbyshire* and her sisters, and their fate. The third and largest piece, the problems of bulk carrier operation, slowly comes into focus as the years pass.

The unravelling of the story of the *Derbyshire* is a complicated task, and we have chosen not to do it in a precisely chronological way but, rather, to look at each of the main elements in turn. These are: the official inquiries, formal and otherwise, culminating in the formal inquiry report of 1989[1] – nine years, note, after the *Derbyshire* sank; the lonely search of Peter Ridyard, a ship's surveyor whose son was on the *Derbyshire*; the fate of the *Kowloon Bridge*; and the research efforts of Professors Bishop, Price and partners.

The first pieces of the jigsaw are the official responses to the loss, starting with the factual statement[2] of May 1981. This unusual step on behalf of the Department of Transport, following the shipping loss, was an eight-page document which started by giving the precise details of the ship and her certificates. The first page, for instance, details her gross tonnage as 91,654.50, her length as 294.1 metres and extreme breadth as 44.28 metres. She was registered in Liverpool and was an OBO 'strengthened' for the carriage of ore cargoes. She had been issued with the following certificates:

Cargo Ship Safety Equipment Certificate issued at Oslo, Norway by Norwegian Administration. Issued 16.4.79, valid to 9.4.81.

Cargo Ship Safety Radio Certificate issued at Sasebo, Japan by Japanese Administration. Issued 16.4.80, valid to 15.4.81.

Cargo Ship Safety Construction Certificate issued by Lloyd's Register, London. Issued 25.10.77, valid to 30.6.81.

International Load Line Certificate issued by Lloyd's Register, London. Issued 14.6.76, valid to 3.6.81, subject to periodical inspection. The last periodical inspection was carried out at Sasebo, 7/15.4.80.

The factual statement continued with a detailing of the *Derbyshire's* navigational equipment: magnetic compass, gyro compass, automatic pilot, two radars, echo sounder, speed log, satellite navigator. Additionally she carried medium, high and very high frequency radio equipment *with a battery source of emergency power of 24 volts DC* (our emphasis). The main aerial was of the cage type and the emergency aerial an inverted ... type. The lifeboat radios were Solas IIIA. The statement says:

> The vessel was drydocked between 7 April and 15 April at Sasebo, Japan where surveyors of Lloyd's Register carried out the annual and docking surveys for classification purposes. To meet the trading programme of the vessel the completion of the classification society's special survey which commenced during this docking was deferred to or before April 1981.[3]

We do not know whether the special survey itself would have shown any problems. The statement points out that 'general examination' of the ship 'proved satisfactory', although it notes that 'Sasebo Heavy Industries carried out *certain* [our emphasis] repair and maintenance work'.[4] We know that this involved the 'veeing' out of the crack around Frame 65, and its repair.

As we know, this crack was first reported in 1977 and it was not suggested then that any structural problem would result. In fact:

> The significance was thought to be that the crack caused a leakage of oil from No. 9 hold into the starboard wing tank. Eventually the crack was repaired but leakage of oil into the starboard cofferdam (see figures in Chapter 10) was not stopped. Since it promised to be a difficult repair to make by reason of inaccessibility, this crack was left until the ship was drydocked in Sasebo . . . in April 1980 . . . In the intervening eight months the crack would grow and, when it was eventually vee'd out and rewelded the damage had become considerable.[5]

The factual statement's description of this is: 'There was a fracture in the bulkhead between No. 9 tank and the pump room and welding was used in the repair. The cofferdams in the engine room were examined internally and found to be clean' (i.e. no leaks).[6]

Much of the statement was concerned with the way the *Derbyshire's* last cargo of iron ore was loaded. This, as we shall see, could have been of significance had, for instance, too much ore been put in one hold rather than another or if iron ore had shifted, or if it had 'liquefied'. The certificates issued from the Canadian port of Sept Iles excluded these possibilities and we may be assured that a Canadian inspector's stamp on a certificate may be relied upon.

Thereafter the statement deals with the typhoon Orchid, and the last messages received from the *Derbyshire*, followed by the search. It notes that although the oil recovered had 'a degree of similarity' to that carried as bunker oil (i.e. fuel) on the *Derbyshire*, the sample was small and sea-water could have affected it. Much more significant was the sighting of the lifeboat and it is worth quoting the statement in full:

On 24 October a Japanese tanker *Taiei Maru* sighted a drifting empty lifeboat in position 21° 14′N, 122° 18′E in the approaches to the Luzon Strait. This position is nearly 700 miles WSW of the position in which oil was seen upwelling on 16 September. This gives a resultant drift of about 1/2 knot over a period of about 44 days. The tanker was unable to recover the lifeboat but it was positively identified as coming from the *Derbyshire* from the name and port of registry on the bow and stern. Damage to the hull extending from gunwale to side bench level was observed near the forward end on the starboard side and one block and part of the fall were still attached to the lifeboat. The lifeboat was flooded to sidebench level and some equipment was observed to be missing.[7]

Did the master of this ship take any photographs – and from how far away? Later this issue becomes crucial for two reasons. The first is that such photographs would prove the validity of the details mentioned in the factual statement; second, they may well enable experts to decide how the lifeboat detached itself from the *Derbyshire*; in particular, was it wrenched free or was some attempt made to launch it? The evidence above suggests that it was wrenched free by the overwhelming force of the sea, as the superstructure sank. In fact someone on board the *Taiei Maru* took a number of photographs, from some distance away and close up.

The factual statement of May 1981 coincides with Lord Trefgarne, then Shipping Minister, telling the House of Lords that he would not be opening a public inquiry. This was on the unanimous advice of his departmental staff. Lord Trefgarne did say however, that he would be prepared to reconsider this decision 'should any new and material evidence come to light'.

Yet we know that behind this unusual statement (all major shipping losses are normally followed by a public inquiry), there were already pressures. The internal, unpublished part of the factual statement contained commentaries on it by senior civil servants and a 'host' of internal memoranda. According to Geoffrey Lean, writing in the *Observer* newspaper much later, 'Officials regarded the inquiry as so secret that the Department's deputy chief surveyor records in one memorandum that he had even "refused to give" the name of the inspector who conducted it (a Mr M. C. Roberts) to a journalist.'[8] This internal report concluded that the disaster could have been due to 'structural hull failure', although it believed the storm was the 'prime cause'. But a comment by Captain Munro in the unpublished report (dated December 1st, 1980) says that the storm 'was not one of the most severe of its kind and *a vessel such as the Derbyshire should have been able to come through it without sustaining anything but relatively superficial damage*'[9] (our emphasis).

Munro said further in his comments that two possibilities emerged from what was known: either an unusual wave formation did the necessary damage, or that might have combined with 'some hitherto undetected weakness in the hull structure' leading to 'the vessel breaking in two and quickly sinking'.[10] He argued that a public inquiry would have to be held, not least because it was normal practice. However, his own boss, the Chief Ship Surveyor, commented elsewhere that 'I cannot see how an investigation in open court could produce any more than could be obtained by our "in-house" researchers'.[11]

It was accepted, publicly and privately, that despite lack of evidence owing to the ship's loss, the matter could not be left there. The *Derbyshire* had been a huge and modern ship crewed by British officers and ratings trained to a high standard. The next report into her loss would state: 'whereas typhoons have accounted for the loss of many ships by their sheer violence, *Derbyshire* was by any standards a large, substantially built ship'.[12] It is to this report we now turn, for it marks the first substantial statement of possible causes of the *Derbyshire's* sinking, which was based on the solid research work of two independent teams. The report was the result of the Department of Transport's own concern about why the *Derbyshire* sank. There had been a meeting of owners and past owners of the ships in her class in London on October 9th, 1980. Its purpose was to try to establish whether these vessels, as a class, suffered from any defect.

According to those present, the operating history of each vessel was thoroughly investigated. The meeting reported to the Department of Transport that 'we were able to establish no evidence of any form of structural weakness in this type of vessel'.[13] It continues: 'As is common with these large vessels there were a number of *minor fractures in the steel works of the holds of each vessel,* but *these do not appear to occur to any pattern* [our emphasis] and in almost every case were the result of *defective welds,* which once made good *did not recur* [our emphasis]'.[14]

By December 1980 three of the ships has suffered cracking at Frame 65: the *Derbyshire,* the *Furness Bridge* and the *Sir Alexander Glen.* It is possible that the *Sir John Hunter* also had had problems at Frame 65 by then.[15] The inspector compiling the initial report on the loss was apprised of the meeting's conclusions and, as a result, saw no reason to widen his inquiries, completed on November 17th, 1980. But:

It was accepted that the matter could not be left there and that there would be a continuing disquiet, certainly among the informed public . . . the Minister . . . decided that this Department should continue its investigations. Of the possible cause of the casualty, a *structural failure seemed to have been the most likely* [our emphasis] and indeed it was the only one which lent itself to the mounting of a detailed investigation.[16]

This official belief that structural failure was the cause comes from the introduction to a draft 'Report into the circumstances attending the loss of the MV *Derbyshire* which foundered about 9 September 1980. It was issued for comments in July 1985.

Under the conclusion it says, *inter alia*:

If *Derbyshire* was constructed in much the same way as the sister ships and there is little reason to suppose she was not, then, in the severe tropical storm which occurred, major cracking possibly developed as it did in *Tyne Bridge.*[17] In the case of the *Derbyshire it is most likely that had cracking taken place it is probable that it took place so rapidly and extensively that total structural failure resulted. This was followed by the capsize of the inhabited portion of the ship abaft Frame 65, this probably accounts for the complete absence of any distress traffic*[18] [our emphasis].

The use of the word 'probable' in this conclusion does not detract from its force. The statement was based not on surmise but on extensive research evidence from two independent academic sources, one of which was the Bishop, Price investigation, and the other, that of the British Ship Research

Association. Both sources – using different methods and unaware of each other's work – concluded structural failure to be the most likely cause for the loss, given certain conditions (which a typhoon would fulfil). This was irrespective of any problems in design or build in the ship, issues to which we shall return.

This must have seemed to those directly involved in 1985 to have wrapped up the whole issue permanently. But draft reports are sent around for comment; and by March 1986, after receiving comments, the report's conclusions were these:

1. Explosion: OBOs of this type have suffered explosions resulting from the carriage of oil. This is less likely in the case of the *Derbyshire* because she had not carried oil since October 1979 . . .

2. Shift of cargo: Engine failure and loss of steerage could bring about a shift of cargo and loss of stability. This could also result from an ingress of water into holds containing a cargo of iron ore thereby causing liquefaction of the cargo.

3. Failure of hatch covers: If hatchcovers are 'sprung', water can enter the holds leading to rapid flooding and foundering. This could happen if the main deck was flexing in a seaway because of the low torsional stiffness of the hull.

4. External hull damage: If the ship struck an uncharted submerged or partially submerged object then the hull could have been penetrated causing ingress of water and loss of stability.

5. Structural hull failure: A failure of part of the hull structure could lead to ingress of water and loss of stability.[19]

This final report rejects the evidence about structural failure ending with the fairly remarkable statement that the *Tyne Bridge* cracking (in 1982, remember) occurred in a ship then ten years old, and was not relevant to the *Derbyshire*: 'In view of [these differences] there is no justification for drawing a parallel between the two ships.' The conclusion, therefore, was that the 'most likely' explanations were as outlined above:

None of them can be entirely eliminated because of the difficulty in pursuing lines of enquiry in the absence of any direct evidence. The fact that no distress signals were received might be thought to support the explanation that massive structural failure was the cause of the loss of the *Derbyshire*. The circumstantial evidence which is described in this report also *tends to point in this direction* [our emphasis] but, in the Department's view, is not itself conclusive. In the last analysis the cause of the loss of *Derbyshire* is, and will almost certainly remain, a matter of speculation'.[20]

A careful reading of these two reports, the draft and the final, shows a number of points in which there has been a reversal of emphasis, and even of conclusions, such as there could be conclusions. The draft report is crystal clear in its sizing up of the evidence on likely causes. After all, the research was commissioned because at least some of the Department of Transport's civil servants believed structural failure was a likely explanation:

In reviewing the cumulative evidence existing from the sister ships what stands out is that all six ships all suffered, to a varying degree, cracking in the vicinity of 65 watertight bulkhead. This includes the *Derbyshire*   It is known that the five remaining ships were constructed differently from the original approved plans in the vicinity of WTB 65.

The alternative method of construction applied was of a simpler character but even then the method of attachment of the longitudinal bulkheads of the topside tanks to the watertight bulkhead at 65 varied in concept and standard of workmanship.

The research work carried out by RINA [Registro Italiano Navale, the Italian classification society; the work was done on the *Tyne Bridge*] showed how significant was the factor of stress concentration induced by the alternative method of construction adopted in *Tyne Bridge*. In our view, this would almost certainly have been present in the four sister ships.

The use of Grade A steel as evidenced in the *Tyne Bridge* may well have extended to the other ships of the class. It meant in fact that the resistance to cracking on account of the factor of heavy stress concentration was lessened.

If *Derbyshire* was constructed in much the same way as the sister ships and there is little reason to suppose that she was not, then in the severe tropical storm which occurred major cracking possibly developed as it did in *Tyne Bridge*.[21]

Between the draft report and the final report, then, a change of emphasis occurred. Even the significance of the BSRA research agreeing with that of Bishop, Price and partners over a structural failure at Frame 65 was not made that prominent in the final report (although their methods of approach had been quite fundamentally different. It is reported that Lloyd's Register had commented that BSRA had had to make many assumptions in respect of fracture strength and applied stresses and that, even if the BSRA work had been more rigorous, there would still have been major assumptions in the analysis.

The draft report has many faults but the thrust of its concern comes out time and time again – and focuses attention not only on the question of structural failure but also on two other vital questions.

There is the relationship between the *Derbyshire* and her sister ships: could parallels be drawn between one ship and another of the same class? To the authors of the draft report the answer was clearly yes. Furthermore the *Tyne Bridge* cracking might be critical to an understanding of the *Derbyshire's* loss, not least because of the possibility of a fracture such as we postulated in our dramatisation (see Chapter 1, p. 6). This brittle fracture happened to *Tyne Bridge*.

The other question is much more disturbing. It concerns the way the ships had been built. By 1984, four years after the *Derbyshire* sank, and two years after the *Tyne Bridge* began to break up, the Department of Transport was in possession of a good deal of information about these ships suggesting that Frame 65 and its surroundings was where the problems lay. This information had come from Lloyd's Register, from the Italian Registro Italiano Navale, from the Liberian Deputy Commissioner of Maritime Affairs and from Peter Ridyard, the marine surveyor.

In July the Department of Transport wrote to Swan Hunter asking for any information they had on the fractures, their likely cause and the repairs found necessary. In addition the shipbuilders were asked for copies of their drawings as approved by Lloyd's Register of Shipping, showing deck and bulkhead structure in the area of Frame 65.

The draft report said:

> The shipbuilders replied on 3 August sending the appropriate drawings. In addition a plan was sent pointing out areas in way of the topside wing tanks and the 'scarphing brackets' on the afterside of the bulkhead at Frame 65 and where the fractures had occurred in some of the sister ships.[22]

They took the opportunity to inform the Department that 'modifications involving additional stiffening were carried out' but that they were *'unable to trace any plans'* (our emphasis). The Department was advised by the shipbuilders to contact Lloyd's Register of Shipping 'who were also involved and should have the relevant information'. The latter caused a search to be made on behalf of the Department *'but no as-built plans of the structure in way of the bulkhead at Frame 65 were available and no explanation can be given'*[23] (our emphasis).

The draft report goes on: 'Thus, there appears to have been a *fundamental departure* [our emphasis] from the approved design connection between the upper wing tank inboard bulkheads (which are also the longitudinal hatch-side girders) and the full height longitudinal bulkheads in the pumproom'[24]. It ends, this 'is surprising . . . and that no record of the change in the approved design has been kept'.[25]

In the final report the statement is edited to: 'there *appeared* [our emphasis] to have been a departure from the approved design . . . ' There is no mention at all of missing plans, but: 'unfortunately the elevation of the construction showing the longitudinal bulkhead 35 feet 6 inches off the centreline, port and starboard was not amended and showed the original design concept . . . ' The final report notes that this led to considerable confusion in assessing how the ships were constructed and whether or not the modification was known to Lloyd's Register and approved by them. Lloyd's had confirmed that, plans or no, the change would have meant that the ships after *Furness Bridge* were of a minimum acceptable standard for classification (unless doubler plates had been fitted, which they would not necessarily have approved in any way).

We have seen that Frame 65 is vital to the whole question of the actual sinking of the *Derbyshire*. But it was not obvious in the days and months after her loss that this particular part of the ship's structure had any significance. As it turned out, the Bishop, Price research identified Frame 65 as the vulnerable point in the after part of these ships. But Bishop's team was deliberately *not* told of the interest by the various parties in Frame 65 in order not to prejudice their work.[26] How then did Frame 65 emerge from the background?

To find that out we now turn to one man's quest for the truth about his son's death. Peter Ridyard's story is one of great tenacity; and, as it was to turn out, of frustration too.

7

The Detective: framing the evidence

Peter and Mavis Ridyard lost a son in the *Derbyshire*. David Ridyard had been the ship's Fourth Engineer. Peter Ridyard wrote in 1985 to Vikki King, whose son Paul was a junior engineer on the *Derbyshire*, that David had always wished in some way to be associated with the sea, 'no doubt this stemming from the fact that seafarers existed on both sides of his family, either in the engineering or catering professions'.

Peter Ridyard managed to get David an apprenticeship with Appledore Shipbuilders in North Devon. When he left there he had gone straight to Bibby Line, joining in 1976. He had sailed in the *Atlantic Bridge, Worcestershire, Ocean Bridge, Hampshire* and finally the *Derbyshire*.

When the ship was lost Peter Ridyard, like everyone else closely associated with her, was devastated. Unlike every other father who lost a son though, Peter was a ship's surveyor with some twenty-eight years experience investigating all types of structural and mechanical marine casualties. This was to prove the most vital single element in the huge effort to get at the truth.

Ship's surveyors come in all shapes and sizes. Peter Ridyard worked for the Salvage Association, a team of marine surveyors representing Lloyd's Underwriters who specialise in assessing damages to vessels on their behalf. His long experience – twenty-seven years – meant that even in the aftermath of the *Derbyshire's* loss his professional antennae were working:

> I felt that because of the type of vessel she was – and rated 100A1 – that it was some kind of structural failure but I knew that I would never be able to prove it. You see, even in a typhoon I would never have anticipated that a ship of that size and strength could have sunk so suddenly. But what could I do. She was at the bottom of the Pacific Ocean. It went out of my head then.

Ridyard had been working in a Salvage Association office in Germany. When his son died the Salvage Association asked if he would like to be transferred home – to Southampton where his wife's family lived. He came home to take over the Southampton office early in 1981. He just carried on, he says.

Part of his work entailed following the passage of shipping casualties, to see if he or his staff would be called in on behalf of underwriters to survey damages to vessels from Newhaven to Falmouth and on the French coast from Dunkirk to Bordeaux which came under his jurisdiction. As part of his job he read Lloyd's casualty reports in *Lloyd's List*, the daily newspaper of the shipping industry:

> I saw then there was a bulk carrier – which turned out to be the *Tyne Bridge* – which had put back into Hamburg for fractures found on the deck. As it was called something *Bridge* I checked it up. I thought there might be a connection with the *Liverpool Bridge* [the *Derbyshire's* first name]. I saw that she was the same class. That rather intrigued me. So what I did then was to contact people in the Blohm and Voss office where I found she was going for repairs. I spoke to the chief estimator, Willy Beck, an old contact and he said, 'Yes, we are dealing with it.' I asked him for the repair list and what they found. He sent it over and then I saw that the repair was all around Frame 65.
>
> That was the first time; that was the start.
>
> The next thing was the *Cast Kittiwake* was coming into Rotterdam with the same problem.

What Peter did not know at that time was that, following the incident with the *Tyne Bridge*, Lloyd's Register had contacted the owners of the other ships in the class and asked them to inspect the area around Frame 65. It was as a result of these inspections that *Cast Kittiwake's* crew found themselves staring at the drydock walls in Rotterdam instead of proceeding on their way.

The principal surveyor for the Salvage Association in Rotterdam phoned Ridyard: 'We've got another one, Peter,' he said. 'Would you like to come across and have a look?' Ridyard went. By the time Peter arrived large chunks of the offending cracked deck and bulkhead had been cut out, some ready to go to Lloyd's Register's research division in Crawley, West Sussex. Ridyard got a piece too.

What Ridyard saw he later described in a letter sent to the General Secretary of the Merchant Navy and Air Line Officers' Association, together with some photographs he had taken:

> I enclose photographs taken of transverse bulkhead crucifix section which was cut away for closer examination and which revealed defects

which could only be described as poor workmanship. It appears that *what should have been a continuous transverse bulkhead with the abutting longitudinal bulkhead and girder was in fact another welded butt on the centre of the crucifix section and under the fitted doubler* or liner. In addition it was found that the numerous transverse floors and brackets where they should have been aligned on either side of the bulkheads were in fact misaligned by up to 50/55mm (two inches).

The Superintendent Surveyor in Rotterdam told Peter that the *Sir Alexander Glen* had gone into a Japanese yard for inspection and that they had found similar defects. 'I knew then that there was a connection,' he says. Using his contacts Ridyard got in touch with another Salvage Association man in Japan. He eventually produced a confidential report for the SA, about the *Sir Alexander Glen*, never produced in public and not called at the formal inquiry (see Chapter 11).

This report confirmed broadly that what Ridyard had seen on the *Cast Kittiwake* was also true of the *Sir Alexander Glen*: misalignment around Frame 65 and the splitting of the longitudinals either side of the bulkhead. By the summer of 1982, then, three of the six ships in the Bridge class had been shown to have major defects in the area of Frame 65, all indicating that poor workmanship was a likely cause in the original building. Peter Ridyard did not know in 1982 that the *Furness Bridge*, first in the class, had been built according to the original approved plans. She did have problems, but never as bad as those of her modified sisters. It was, however, as a result of the series of incidents in 1982 that urgent remodifications were carried out on three (*Tyne Bridge, Cast Kittiwake* and *Sir Alexander Glen*) of the remaining four modified ships – effectively returning them to the original design (see figures in Chapter 10).

The *English Bridge* did not report any problems at the time. It is worth remembering that in the absence of deck cracking it was hard to get at the area of Frame 65 outside of drydocking. We now know that when the *Kowloon Bridge* (as she became) went down she had not had these vital remodifications; the concession to Frame 65 had been the two welded girders on her deck (see Chapter 8).

In 1982 Peter Ridyard's reaction to what he had found was to write to the Department of Transport. He was invited to London to talk to two of their officials, Mr Noble and Mr Gilbert. Ridyard remembers saying that they should contact the Salvage Association. He also advised them to go to Japan where the *Sir Alexander Glen* was still being repaired and where, Ridyard now knew, the *Derbyshire* had been found to have a fracture around Frame 65 in her last survey in April 1980. They went.

But then, silence fell. Peter felt increasingly frustrated. He now had the Italian classification society's report[1] on the *Tyne Bridge*. From this he realised that the ship's longitudinal girders had been terminated at bulkhead 65; that there had been substantial misalignment between this longitudinal girder and the longitudinal on forward and after bulkhead on the afterside of bulkhead 65. This further proof of misalignment had disturbed the classification society, RINA, and they had insisted on the modification which 'clipped' the section of the girder just forward and the longitudinal bulkhead aft of no. 65 bulkhead, slotting no. 66 bulkhead and welding in a new section of girder so that it became continuous with the longitudinal bulkheads, in other words, securing the front of the ship to its rear.

Ridyard knew by the autumn of 1983, a whole year on, that the Department of Transport had commissioned at least one research organisation to look into possible causes of the *Derbyshire's* loss. He believes this meant that the Department told the British Ship Research Association to investigate possible structural failures. They subsequently commissioned Bishop, Price and Temarel to do the same, using a completely different method (see Chapter 9, p. 77).

A former colleague wrote to Peter in November 1983: 'The Department of Transport, like all Government organisations, is slow to move but I believe they make exhaustive inquiries and when these are completed, as they may be in this case, I will be very surprised if a formal inquiry is not ordered.' He added:

> Peter, your research into the matter can do little to help in your personal loss and sorrow. However, I am sure that you are motivated by the desire for more stringent regulations for safety of life at sea.[2]

Also in November came a letter which caused Peter and Mavis Ridyard only grief. It came from the solicitors acting for the officers' union (MNAOA) and said they felt there was no purpose in pursuing any party to the loss of the *Derbyshire* through the courts. There had been a request to extend the time limit on legal action to December but the feeling was that this would not help. This letter triggered an immediate response from Peter Ridyard. Instructing his own solicitors, they wrote to the Merchant Navy union solicitors on November 28th, pointing out what Ridyard had discovered. Among other things they asked:

> Were any inquiries made by investigators re. the serious structural failures in sister vessels to the *Derbyshire* each of which were constructed at Swan Hunter Shipbuilders Ltd, Haverton Hill, Sunderland?

Has any approach been made by the investigators to examine the *Tyne Bridge* until recently owned by Sicula Oceanica, Palermo, Italy, the *Cast Kittiwake* managed by Denholm Ship Management, Glasgow, also the *Sir Alexander Glen* managed by the same firm?

The sending of this letter, and the subsequent rekindling of interest by the various parties to the loss, had enormous ramifications. Indeed in our view there was an inevitable relationship between the subsequent difficulties in getting at material and the sending of this letter. One of the saddest aspects of the whole story has been the lament, often heard by relatives, that any chance of getting to the truth of this complex technical matter of shipbuilding and design was lost once legal processes were engaged. To some extent that is true. The lawyers' interest was legal: gathering enough evidence to sue someone. The relatives, at least early on, wanted something quite different: justice and, through it, peace of mind. Money was never the priority. But the involvement of lawyers meant that many of the relatively neutral parties were forced to take positions and were soon refraining from saying too much or, worse, refusing to hand over documents and papers.

Some things still surprised Peter though, as they might anyone looking at this story. On December 1st, 1983 the MNOAO solicitors, Ingledew, Brown, Bennison and Garrett, wrote to Peter's that: 'The Department of Transport have not obtained from Lloyd's Register details of cracking problems of sister ships nor recommended modifications. The ships in question were under *foreign flag at the material time and apparently the Department have felt that they had no proper authority to request this information*' [our emphasis].[3] This was, in any case, not accurate. Only the *Tyne Bridge* was under a foreign flag at the time; the rest were British registered.

By January 1984, Ingledew *et al.* were writing directly to Peter: 'Far from carrying out a proper, if informal inquiry, the Department appear to have limited their inquiries purely to the basic design of the *Derbyshire* . . . '[4]

At the same time, any legal proceedings were likely to come up against the classic problem of being beyond the time limit. However, Belinda Bucknall, Admiralty Counsel, consulted by Ingledew and partners, told them that as the cracking in the sister ships of the *Derbyshire* had occurred nearly two years after the ship had been lost, this might weigh in their favour. She advised that it was vital that the evidence of cracking in all four sister ships be collected. On this basis they could proceed.

In 1984 Peter Ridyard believed they were well on their way to getting the answers to the loss of the *Derbyshire* made public. But the key to the legal case lay in getting accurate information. The world of shipping is the most international of all businesses. As we have already seen, its personnel

travel and work all over the globe. Ships too change hands with be-
wildering speed; they can be managed in one country but flagged in
another, insured somewhere else, repaired wherever they happen to be,
crewed likewise. Getting information depends on contacts – and luck.

Ridyard was well placed to get the data. His telex of March 1984 says it all:

Loss of *Derbyshire* Sept 1980. Have been making personal investigations
into loss of this vessel of which six of the same class were constructed at
Haverton Hill. I have obtained information of serious constructional
defects in three of these vessels in way of the No. 65 transverse bulkhead
and longitudinal slop tank bulkhead which continues to the No. 5 upper
wing tank bulkhead as a result of which fractures originated at the after
corners of No. 9 hatch coaming. There are two vessels I have not been
able to obtain information on these being the *English Bridge* now in the
Far East and the *Furnace Bridge* [*Furness Bridge*] now called the *Marcona
Pathfinder* and owned by the Utah Transport inc 550 California Street
San Francisco. In order to establish whether all five sister ships had the
same 'built in' defects I would very much appreciate if you could make
inquiries with this company on my behalf if they know of any defects
found in this area on the *Marcona Pathfinder*. Lloyd's Register, after
serious defects were found in another sister vessel the *Cast Kittiwake*,
issued a directive for additional strengthening in this area and possibly
the *Marcona Pathfinder* was similarly dealt with . . . solicitors in London
acting for the Merchant Navy and Air Line Officers' Association have
informed me that they have written to Utah Transport, however I feel
that it is possible that 'we do not wish to get involved' attitude might
result and therefore a diplomatic approach by you to, say, the port
engineer may be more rewarding.

This telex was sent to the Salvage Association's San Francisco office. No reply
is recorded. Meanwhile Peter was trying to jolly along the Department
of Transport. In a long letter to Lord Campbell of Croy, who had raised the
issue of the *Derbyshire* in the House of Lords in May 1981, Ridyard sets
out the chronology of all his efforts. The letter is dated July 17th 1984.
Lord Trefgarne, then Shipping Minister, had said there was no point in
having a public inquiry at that time because there was so little evidence.
But it had been around this time that the Department of Transport had
commissioned their own research. Trefgarne had said that if new evidence
came to light he would reconsider the decision over a public inquiry.

Ridyard's letter points out that the new evidence was now available. He

tells Lord Campbell about the *Tyne Bridge* and the *Cast Kittiwake* and
continues:

In September 1982 I became aware of similar defects in the *Sir Alexander
Glen* as a consequence of which I wrote to the Department of Trade
informing them of my findings. I received a letter dated September 22nd
stating that my letter was being studied and they would respond in due
course. In June 1983 I again wrote to the Department of Trade referring
to my previous letter, to be informed on July 19th that the report of the
British Ship Research Association was inconclusive and that they were
funding a second stage of research by the BSRA.

They had then received a second report and would be writing to me
again. I did not have another letter until June 27th, 1984 . . . I ultimately
contacted my MP, Sir David Price, who took the matter up with the
Minister of Shipping after which I received a copy of a letter written by
the Minister to Sir David in which he stated that the Department of Trade
had done as much as it reasonably could to ensure that no other British
seamen's lives are lost as a consequence of defects similar to any that
may have been in the *Derbyshire*.

I replied . . . to the effect that in my view the Department had not
investigated the possible defects in three sister vessels in fact I was aware
that no approach had been made to the owners of these other vessels or
even to examine a sample of the defective welding found on the *Cast
Kittiwake* and retained in the Salvage Association office in Rotterdam.

In August 1984 Peter Ridyard received a different kind of letter. It was from
Vikki King, mother of Paul, who asked if he could help in her own search
for the truth behind the sinking. Slowly the families were beginning to stir.
It was out of this stirring, and the gathering legal actions, that the *Derbyshire*
Families Association was to be formed (Vikki King became its chairman).
Mavis and Peter Ridyard were to become friends of Vikki and Des King as
the months and then years rolled on. Peter's reply to Vikki had been
characteristically vigorous and positive. He told her he had built a model of
the *Derbyshire* which showed the defects, and would be more than happy to
show it to her.

A Mr Harvey of the Department of Transport finally wrote to Peter in
September 1984:

You will be interested to hear that our Mr Noble [a principal ship
surveyor in the Department] has recently returned from a visit to Japan.
During his visit he was given every assistance by your Mr Wilcox and

also by Mr H. MacNeill, senior principal surveyor for Lloyd's Register of Shipping in Japan. He was able to gather useful information on the *Derbyshire* and some of the sister ships, which will help in our investigations.

Also we have now received permission from the owners of the *Sir Alexander Glen* and the *Cast Kittiwake* to have copies made of certain documents held by Mr Galloway at your London office.[5]

Time dragged on. Peter continued his researches on all fronts, now contacting the Italians for details on the *Tyne Bridge* faults and repairs, now asking a friend (a lifeboat expert) to look into the photograph of the *Derbyshire's* lifeboat and to give an opinion on how the damage might have been caused. But after the one letter from the Department of Transport there was more silence.

In March 1985 Vikki King wrote to Prime Minister Margaret Thatcher. It was a brave letter, but, as all such letters must be, the cry of a woman who had begun to feel that despite all the work by Peter Ridyard, nothing was actually happening. Vikki King ended her letter: 'You who know the fear when told a son is missing can imagine the despair when a husband or son is not found. Can imagine too the feelings when it appears that no one cares. A formal inquiry would show that the government of that day does care . . . Please help.'

The circulation of the long-awaited Department of Transport report (discussed in Chapter 6) was not greeted with much enthusiasm by Peter. Although, five years on, and after the factual statement, its conclusions seem to be fairly devastating, Peter took the view that it did not go far enough in blaming those he considered guilty. By then he was a direct party to the legal action started on behalf of the Merchant Navy Union, an action which was bound, perhaps, to fail. While in April 1985 Ingledew and partners were discussing 'the possibility of proving that building defects found in sister ships may also have been present in *Derbyshire* and were perhaps responsible for her loss', Peter already felt sure that he *knew*. Five years after the disaster, and three after his own introduction to the 'defects', he more than anyone had investigated the ships and their building.

Most important, he had now realised that at least one of the ships had not been built according to the original plans. Writing to Ingledew and partners in June 1985, he said:

One vital fact that has to be established is why the series of vessels were not constructed in accordance with details shown in the scantling plans

. . . The original drawings would have been drawn by the shipbuilders, approved by the owners and rendered to Lloyd's Register for their approval. If at the building stage a radical change in design in the region of No. 65 bulkhead was proposed, this must have been approved by the classification surveyor on site, and, being in such a high-stress area, the local plans approval department should have given their approval if Head Office were not informed.

Ridyard said that the BSRA original report to the Department of Transport had concluded that the kind of construction found in the *Tyne Bridge* and the others could have exacerbated general stress in the area of Frame 65. But, he added, he had not been able to find out whether the same construction had applied to the *English Bridge*.[6]

By July he had had a copy of the draft Department of Transport report with all the BSRA and the Bishop, Price research included. He wrote to thank Mr Gilbert at the Department of Transport for sending it and detailing what he considered to be vital errors in it. But he added:

A comment I would make on the *Furness Bridge* which may be of significance. If one refers to the Lloyd's Register Report No. 20068 in appendix 6, sheet 8 under heading *Marcona Pathfinder* (ex *Lake Arrowhead*) and to paragraph under sub-heading 1.8 we note as follows: 'Longitudinal bulkhead plating of No. 5 topside tanks port and starboard fractured 450mm down from the upper deck where *scarphed through* [his emphasis] transverse bulkhead No. 65.' Later, under 'Now Done' I note that E grade steel was used in the renewal of the No. 65 bulkhead and sloping bottom plating of the No. 65 topside tanks etc. Does not the foregoing [indicate] the possibility that the first constructed vessel could well have had a continuous longitudinal through the No. 65 bulkhead.

This was to be the turning point in his investigation for, up to that point, Peter had had no idea that the ships had not all been built like the *Furness Bridge* with the longitudinals continuing through the 65 bulkhead.

This was to prove so. The *Furness Bridge* was built to plan.[7] Because of an International Maritime Organisation rule a cofferdam was introduced between the No. 9 hold and the pump room, aft. As the drawings show, this meant a considerable complication of local design, and an increased difficulty of access. (See figures in Chapter 10.) This difficulty of access experienced in the building of the *Furness Bridge* meant that a change was made in the way all the other five ships were built. This is the crucial design change because it meant cutting the longitudinals, their continuance now dependent on an exact alignment either side of the No. 65 bulkhead. Peter Ridyard, after three years of detective work, had finally established the change in design between the first ship of the series and the rest.

In their draft report of 1985 the Department of Transport had referred to this when they said it remained inexplicable that neither Swan Hunter nor Lloyd's Register could find the plans of this major, and, as Peter says, 'radical' change. It was to restore an approximation to the original that the work on *Tyne Bridge*, *Cast Kittiwake* and *Sir Alexander Glen* was done in 1982. This is important. When the formal inquiry inspected the *Sir Alexander Glen* they could reasonably pronounce her Frame 65 arrangement satisfactory. By 1987 of course it was: the modifications had been in place for five years. Only three ships in 1985 had not been modified to make them stronger: *Furness Bridge* did not need changing; the *Derbyshire* was sunk; and the last, *English Bridge*, was not yet ready to make her own dramatic entry into the story. That was to be a year later, in the autumn of 1986.

To our mind, one of the more depressing aspects of this story is the slow progress made towards the light. Peter Ridyard believed in 1985, after the draft Department of Transport report had arrived, that they were finally moving in the right direction. But when in another six months he got to read the final report, which, as we have seen, watered down the conclusions of the draft report, he despaired.

He had done all he could to provide relevant facts about all the ships. His work had been painstaking (and expensive in terms of time and money). He had in fact carried out a most impressive piece of detective work and his evidence was concise. Yet it seemed that no one in authority was going to act on it.

Then in the autumn of 1986 Peter Ridyard heard of another bulker in dire trouble. Anchored in Bantry Bay on the south-east coast of Ireland, she was the *Kowloon Bridge*. 'Can you get me on a flight to Cork?' he asked his secretary.

8

The Ship that Died of Shame

By 1986 Peter Ridyard's long, lonely fight was beginning to pay off, or at least he thought it was. The evidence had grown enormously that the most likely explanation for the loss of the *Derbyshire* was structural failure at Frame 65. There had been the Bishop, Price and Temarel research, the BSRA work, even the watered-down version of the DoT report. And there had been the evidence of the *Tyne Bridge* and the *Cast Kittiwake* (ex-*Sir John Hunter*).

In September 1986 Roger Stott, then Shadow Minister for Transport, headed a delegation of unions in a meeting with the government Shipping Minister, Lord Brabazon. Stott explained the developments since 1982 and all the evidence that had now been accumulated. He appealed, on behalf of all the interested parties, for a formal inquiry. Lord Brabazon listened but would not commit himself. Not long after this meeting, in November, Stott received a letter from Brabazon turning down his suggestion. He had hardly finished reading the letter for a second time when an excited aide interrupted his thoughts. 'Another of the *Derbyshire* class ships is in trouble,' he said, 'this time off the coast of Ireland.'

The *Kowloon Bridge*, formerly the *English Bridge* and third in the series, was built to the 'modified' plan. In 1986 she was the only remaining ship which had not been remodified. In this sense we believe it is reasonable to assume the *Derbyshire* was exactly like her.

She had had several name changes since *English Bridge* – *Mercurio, Crystal Transporter, Sunshine* and now *Kowloon Bridge*. On this voyage she had been transporting 160,000 tons of iron ore from Canada to the Ravenshead iron ore berth on the Clyde, and according to her Indian master, Captain Reo, she had had a bad Atlantic crossing. As she struggled along the coast of southern Ireland her radio calls were heard by Captain Byrne, the master of a nearby coaster. Reo was calling a London number – probably his managers or agents. He told them that he had now anchored safely (in Bantry Bay), and how relieved he was to have reached this point of relative safety. In his opinion the ship was no longer seaworthy. He asked for an inspection to assess the damage.

Captain Byrne's account was part of a BBC Radio Four *Face the Facts* programme on the *Derbyshire*. He said: 'The damage [reported] consisted of damage to a frame in No. 9 hold, and the captain indicated that because of that damage, he felt the ship was unseaworthy. My impression of the captain at the time was that he was very relieved to be out of the weather.' We know that newspaper clippings about the *Derbyshire* were later found in his cabin and we may guess at what he was thinking.

The subsequent survey apparently showed only 'routine heavy weather damage' and repairs began on the anchored ship. But fate now took a hand and in deteriorating weather the anchor cable parted. Captain Reo had no choice but to leave his restricted anchorage and put to sea. He must have had a heavy heart as he did so; a storm was forecast. We do not know how quickly he left Bantry Bay, or whether the ship's spurling pipes had been covered (to stop water pouring into the anchor locker). We do not know, therefore, how the ship was handling; or whether there were problems in steering her. Captain Reo, despite numerous attempts to trace him, has not been found since this incident.

On November 22nd at 11.05 p.m. the *Kowloon Bridge* was only ten miles from Bantry Bay when Captain Reo ordered a distress message to be transmitted when 'the bow crashed into the sea and did not appear to come back up'. According to contemporary accounts in the *Daily Telegraph*, 'Her Indian master sent out a Mayday call saying she was taking in water and her steering had failed . . . "All I can say is that the problems occurred immediately and were caused by heavy weather conditions," he said.'[1]

By a coincidence two RAF SAR helicopters were at Cork, refuelling after operations involving a pair of Spanish trawlers, and they were soon over the *Kowloon Bridge*. The first to arrive lifted fourteen of the Turkish and Indian crew to safety. The second helicopter moved in to complete the rescue.

As RAF Sergeant Barry Hunter was being lowered on the winch wire, 'the ship came up and bit me,' as he put it. It must have been a terrifying experience dangling beneath the helicopter, struggling to stay steady in winds gusting at 75 knots, the deck of this gigantic ship rising and falling beneath. It was as he swung helplessly that the hatchside slammed into him, breaking bones in his left hand and badly jarring his elbow. Pausing only long enough to get his breath back, he set about attaching the frightened crew on the deck to the hoist, two at a time. His winch operator, Sergeant David Spain, hauled them up.

The distress message was sent at 11.05; only two hours later twenty-eight men were standing on the tarmac at Cork. It had been a record-breaking Air-Sea rescue.

The *Kowloon Bridge* was now abandoned as an account from another seafarer, Captain P. J. Walsh of Cork, relates:

When I switched off my bedside light that Sunday night she was just outside the harbour entrance and not very far from my bungalow, a ship with 165,000 tons of cargo and no crew on board; one that had been allowed to drift for the previous twenty-four hours with absolutely no attempt being made to board her.

Walsh, who had himself been nine hours adrift in a liferaft after a sinking, continued:

While I slept she continued her eastward drift, passing the entrance to Baltimore harbour so close that her great bulk dominated the night skyline, offering all the people who ventured down a sight never to be forgotten. Before drifting past she just missed grounding on Sherkin Island. A navy vessel in attendance reported she would finally end up on Kedge Island, just beyond Baltimore.

Their predictions were very much in contrast to the course she was now taking as she carried on with her drift for a further four hours.

Shortly after 3 a.m. on November 25th the *Kowloon Bridge* hit the Stag Rocks. Captain Walsh tells how the little village of Baltimore was besieged by newsmen and rubber-neckers looking for the ship. Then it dawned on them that the only way they were going to see her was by a six-mile boat trip to the east.

Over the next four days the spotlight turned on this huge ship, stranded well and truly. Two powerful salvage tugs from that acknowledged nation of salvage experts, Holland, tried to shift her but the rocks held on. If the Dutch salvage crews could not get her off, it was fairly clear no one would.

During the first week after her grounding the weather was fine – in fact divers could work safely in and around the vessel. Boats were brought alongside and many local fishermen did what others have done in their time: stole aboard to help themselves to items for 'safekeeping'. Some of these items were later impounded by Irish customs officers. But while this was going on her bunker oil was now threatening to pollute the waters. As with her drifting, which no one in authority seemed capable of preventing, after the tugs had failed to move her, she was just left. Soon south-westerly gales began to blow in, one after another. The *Kowloon Bridge* broke into three. How she sank – that is, the points at which she broke in three – are crucial to the story of the *Derbyshire*. But before we deal with these details of the ship's final foundering, we must divert our attention to a ship lying in Rotterdam, named *East Bridge*.

It was April 1987 and the wreck of the *Kowloon Bridge* had been bought for a nominal £1 by a man called Shaun Kent, a scrap metal merchant.

By that time the *Kowloon Bridge* had already caused the Irish government and fishermen grief by the spillage of her bunker oil, which spread along the coast for over seventy miles. The Irish government declared an exclusion zone of 1000 metres around the wreck and an attempt was made to recover the remaining oil. Shaun Kent and his team of divers had been involved indirectly in these operations, removing a number of barrels of toxic paint from the shipwreck. Kent was eager to get on with his salvage work and he sent a man called Jim Gray, contracted to Kent's company, Copy Logic, to Rotterdam to inspect the *East Bridge* in order to compare this ship with their wreck. For the *East Bridge* was a sister of the *Kowloon Bridge*. We have met her before as the *Tyne Bridge*.

When Gray got to see her in Rotterdam, he was appalled:

The main crack was eight to ten feet long on the port side near to No. 1 hold (forward). The top four feet were gaping open far enough to put your hand through. The top and bottom of the crack had been drilled (to stop it propagating further). There were other, hairline, cracks. After seeing her I would not have sailed in her.[2]

This news about the *East Bridge* reached Jim Slater, then president of the National Union of Seamen. On behalf of relatives of the crew, Slater had been a leading member of the *Derbyshire* campaign. He saw at once what the problems of the *East Bridge* could mean and asked the Department of Transport for inspectors to go out and see her. Subsequently they did, as did surveyors from Lloyd's, but we do not know what they reported. Slater, however, bearing in mind the events surrounding the sinking of *Kowloon Bridge*, took decisive action. He asked the International Transport Workers Federation to try to hold *East Bridge* in Setubal, Portugal, her next port of call. As it turned out, this was academic. In 1989 the *East Bridge*, née *Tyne Bridge*, was sailing on her last voyage to Taiwan, where she was scrapped. Whatever their surveyors may have reported, Lloyd's themselves acted quickly. They had stated that cracks that were known about in the *Kowloon Bridge*, before she sailed from Canada, were not in their opinion likely to lead to her sinking. But after seeing the *East Bridge* cracks they urgently warned the owners of the *Cast Kittiwake* and the *Sir Alexander Glen*, as noted in Chapter 4.

[73]

The research of the Bishop, Price and Temarel team recognised two areas in a ship's hull where additional stresses might be found: one, towards the stern, roughly coincides with Frame 65; two coincides with the area right forward, about number one hold. The cracks in the *East Bridge*, as seen by Jim Gray, are consistent with these theoretical predictions.

What though, of the *Kowloon Bridge*? She had struck Stag Rocks between number two and number three holds, fairly far forward. The holds flooded and the hull broke at this point. She was thus suspended at her forward end and remained in that condition for about five days. She was slowly sinking as water got into the engine room and the void spaces between the holds. Gradually the engine room (aft) became submerged. The weather at this time remained fine. Divers were working in the ship. As Peter Ridyard estimated, 'there would have been about 11,000 tonnes of water in the engine room and the pump room spaces. However, this was a static loading and as the hull in way of Frame 65 bulkhead was not impaled on rocks the stress could not have been abnormal.'

But when she broke at her after end *Kowloon Bridge* ripped all the way round Frame 65.

She had suffered a good deal already, much in this area:

April–May 1982   cracking repaired in starboard wing tank in way of Frame 65

October 1985   an unauthorised repair in this area was made

February 1986   permanent and minor repair made at number one hold side tank plating, starboard side, aft end

May 1986   small fractures repaired near Frame 65, repairs 'permanent'

August 1986   crack in main deck near Frame 65; plating cropped and renewed. Recurrence of cracking elsewhere near Frame 65. Cracks veed out and rewelded. Two fabricated T section stiffeners welded to main deck

The Lloyd's Report (out of Fremantle, Australia)[3] says that 'It appeared that cracking was in May 1986 and that damage was now much more serious than in May.'

October 1986   ultrasonic tests reveal cracking in welds in way of bulkhead 65

November 1986   cracking and rippling of main deck and cracking
                 below deck. Surveyors outlined temporary repairs
                 which were needed before the ship could complete
                 her voyage; temporary repairs were made by the
                 crew.

Captain Reo was assured that this damage did not make the ship structurally unsound. We may surmise that he was adding a few grey hairs as
his ship crossed the Atlantic in 'difficult' conditions. The Department
of Transport surveyor who had come aboard during the time he was
anchored had reported that: 'there was no evidence of any defect in design
of direct link with structural failure which occurred on the sister ship *Tyne
Bridge*, or the cracking found in other sister vessels or with the speculation
surrounding possible failure of the *Derbyshire* at Frame 65'.[4]

And yet, it was the sinking of the *Kowloon Bridge* which finally triggered
the government into ordering a formal inquiry, which began late in 1987.
But we shall see that although the *Kowloon Bridge* sinking *directly* led to this
inquiry, at the inquiry little time was spent on discussing the *Kowloon
Bridge*, her destruction or its relevance to any of the other Bridge class ships,
especially the *Derbyshire*.

The *Kowloon Bridge* is perhaps the most crucial element in the story. She
had been suffering from bad cracking in way of Frame 65; she had been in
bad weather; she was carrying iron ore. She sank in such a way that we
have real, hard evidence of the weakness of Frame 65 and the bulkhead
arrangements. There is video film of this shipwreck showing how she split
at this point.

But worries over weakness of structure is still only a part of the story. The
more alarming, because it relates to all bulk carriers (and possibly tankers
above a certain size), is the issue of dynamic ship stresses, and how these
may lead to additional stresses at portions of a ship's hull not conventionally strengthened to take account of them. A weak structure at either of
these points would enhance the chances of failure if a ship was built badly
or with poor materials or poor welding, or met extreme weather. The
theory of dynamic stress has been the long-term research of the Bishop,
Price and Temarel team. Its work – in part, remember, commissioned by
the Department of Transport – is vital to the jigsaw puzzle we are trying to
complete. To that research work, and its findings, we now turn.

9

Hardening Truths

While Peter Ridyard and others laboured to find the evidence to prove how the *Derbyshire* was lost, others had been working more generally on the problems of large ship stresses, including those of bulk carriers. Some of this work had been continuing since 1974.

Professor Richard Bishop and Professor Geraint Price, along with Dr Pandelli Temarel are the key actors in one strand of this research. Their field is hydro-elasticity, a highly technical subject involving complex mathematics and much computer work. But their results can be understood by anyone.

In the aftermath of the loss of the *Derbyshire* the Department of Transport commissioned research into why the ship had sunk. Eventually that research was to involve Professor Bishop and his partners, as well as the British Ship Research Association. The Department of Transport was anxious to get these two groups to investigate the structural strength of the *Derbyshire* – which was the central contention: 'It was important that, as a minimum, two separate organisations should carry out these investigations into the structural design of the ship,'[1] An added consideration was whether the research would expose possible weaknesses in the design, a prescient question, given what was later discovered by Ridyard.

Thus the Department asked the BSRA in July 1981 to review ship design and operation and existing design calculations; to calculate whether the design calculations were consistent with the last known loading data for *Derbyshire*; to provide a full ship's motion analysis, with a 'representative' sea state; and a hull girder bending shear and torsional analysis with both still water and motion-induced forces (concentrating on the cargo hold length); to review observed areas of minimum margins of safety, fatigue characteristics and brittle fracture propagation, and extreme motions; along with a number of other elements which may have been involved.

This part of the research, as it turned out, did not yield anything of significance. A second stage of BSRA research began in 1983. This was after the incidents involving the *Tyne Bridge* and the other ships and, much more significantly, after the Department of Transport had had discussions with

Peter Ridyard. In many ways then, Peter Ridyard can be said to have initiated the rest of the research programme. The BSRA were now asked additionally to look at:

1 Ship's motions – roll response and torsion. Determine the maximum hull girder torques, assuming range of sea states, range or radius of gyrations, and probable effects on shifted cargo.
2 Simulation of ship's motions using hybrid computer. Assess the behaviour of the vessel in an adverse sea state with shifting cargo and identify conditions which could lead to instability.
3 Torsional analysis of hull girder. Carry out a three-dimensional analysis of the hull girder under a torsional load and identify highly-stressed areas and their probable failure mode.
4 Torsional-horizontal bending vibration study. Carry out a vibration assessment, with the hull girder torsional properties adjusted to emulate the response calculated in the three-dimensional analysis.
5 Green seas. Estimate the loading caused by shipping green seas and the effect of this on forward structure and hatch covers.
6 Detailed strength analysis. Assess the combined effect of the above studies.[2]

This work was finished by the summer of 1983. The main conclusion of that part dealing with 'overall structural integrity' was that the 'hull girder'[3] should have been able to withstand the forces associated with significant wave heights of up to 18 metres (close to 60 feet) due to head or oblique seas with the possibility of only a modest amount of buckling damage. But the report of the BSRA went on to predict what might have happened if waves of up to 30 metres (100 feet) had been encountered – as was reported by the *Alrai* in the same severe storm as *Derbyshire*. The report suggested 'major damage being incurred leading possibly to progressive failure. If major hull girder damage had occurred then the region of the deck between the superstructure and the aft quarter point is likely to have been the *initial* [our emphasis] site.'[4] This puts us near Frame 65.

A good deal of the analyses carried out in the standard way do not take account of the relative motions of ships in water – the dynamic stresses. And they do not give equal weight to shearing forces, as opposed to the weight given to bending forces. Again, in the complex arguments about the way the *Derbyshire* may have sunk, this is a critical distinction. The work undertaken by Bishop, Price and partners in July 1983 involved a separate and independent study of the structural strength of the *Derbyshire*. The Department of Transport report on this research says: 'It can best be described as a dynamic analysis of the horizontal and vertical responses based on the loading and the structural design of the *Derbyshire* to assess the possibility of a structural response causing failure of the hull.'[5]

The research calculated the natural frequencies of symmetric dry hull distortion; the resonance frequencies of symmetric wet hull distortion; the natural frequencies of antisymmetric dry hull distortion; principal modes of the dry hull; vertical responses (of distortion, bending moment, shearing force at any point in the hull in the form of a computer simulation for the ship travelling in an idealised typhoon-generated seaway); stresses in vertical response at any point along the hull.

The results were ready by the summer of 1984. The Department of Transport says:

> The report in coming to certain conclusions did cast much doubt on the conventional methods of assessing hull strength . . . reasons are given for suspecting that the hull may have suffered gross fatigue in the general area of the forward extremity of the superstructure . . . The forward extremity of the superstructure occurred at Frame 67 [*sic*]. It will be recalled that BSRA in their report postulated the possible site of major hull girder damage occurring between the superstructure and the aft one quarter point as the most likely. This would be about Frame 89.[6]

By 1984 then, the Department had two research reports, from completely separate sources using completely different methods, but coming to the same fundamental conclusion. To spell that out – as the exact nature of the formula is critical – in a *well-built and properly designed* (our emphasis) ship of this class, given certain sea and weather conditions, there is great vulnerability in the area around number nine hold (the area which incorporates Frame 65).

We have also seen that by the time the Department of Transport issued the final version of the report in 1986, although based on these research efforts, the conclusions had been watered down considerably; as had their own assessment of what the research, along with the evidence from the ships of the class still sailing, all pointed to. It is worth noting too that Bishop, Price and partners did not know about the *Tyne Bridge* and the rest. When they finally met Peter Ridyard and his researches he gave them the section of *Cast Kittiwake* to work on.

Professors Bishop and Price's work had remained outside the traditional analyses of ship strength and weaknesses, but its importance has never been in doubt. Shipping remains a traditional industry and it moves slowly. In this case accepting the general concept would involve a radical rethinking of ship design and building. Nevertheless by the autumn of 1991 Lloyd's Register researchers had fitted strain gauges to the decks of all the P and O bulk carriers in operation, amidships (the classic position) and at the break of the deck and superstructure (the Frame 65 position on *Derbyshire*).

Why then did the Bishop, Price and partners' research identify this area as crucial? They had no knowledge, remember, of this being a problem area on any of these ships.

The best explanation of what they had been studying came in the RINA paper, read by Professor Price in October 1990, at the meeting described in Chapter 2. The analysis divided the ship into fifty equal slices and the dry hull was treated as a conventional Timoshenko beam, though no allowance was made for the probably very small effects of rotatory inertia. They assumed the whole hull was constructed of mild steel. The typhoon generation was a problem: 'the complicated interaction between the wind and seas is practically impossible to express mathematically'[7] But they came up with a uniform 'severe' seaway – far less of a storm-tossed ocean, we can be sure, than the *Derbyshire* encountered. Putting the two together they simulated the ship moving ahead at 5.25 knots in a head sea. They allowed for 'impact and momentum bottom slamming, though its effects were very small'.[8]

Previously the team had done research work on the Japanese ship *Onomichi Maru* which had broken up towards the bow in heavy weather but had stayed afloat. An analysis of the results had shown that ships are not only stressed amidships but at two other points. These are about 25 per cent from the forward end (the point which broke in the *Onomichi Maru*) and about 15 per cent from the after end (around Frame 65 in the *Derbyshire*). The immensely complex analysis of the simulations came to this:

The analysis is one of field stresses. It makes no allowance for local stress concentration. Such concentrations are certain to exist and any local defect will enhance the stresses that are calculated. Where the calculated stresses are large, any local defect of design or construction or in the material can be expected to have a *disproportionately large effect* [our emphasis].[9]

The paper then turned to the whole class of ships. It was after Bishop, Price and partners had reported their initial work on the *Derbyshire* that they heard about Frame 65, not before: 'We learned . . . that just in the region we had referred to, there may have been a structural defect which could have had a profound effect on the *Derbyshire*'s ability to tolerate the responses . . . The suspected defect was at Frame 65, just forward of the superstructure.'[10] It then went into the details of how the area of Frame 65 had been built, modified, and then modified again; and pointed out that if significant misalignment was found in all the other ships, it would be reasonable to suppose the *Derbyshire* had had the same problems:

> The significance of the misalignment is a matter for debate. The conclusion that has to be drawn . . . is that it could constitute the source of fatigue cracks by reason of high local stresses and that those cracks could well propagate. The 'traditional' view is that 'any misalignment of the inboard vertical side of the topside tank with the pump room longitudinal bulkhead at transverse bulkhead 65 is significant only for local strength aspects'. This disagreement is really quite central.[11]

Then it looked at the issues of fatigue cracking. It is well-attested phenomena that all large ships may have cracks at various stress points in their hulls. These cracks, common to welded ships (as opposed to the old-fashioned, riveted ships) may develop (propagate) or not. Sometimes, to stop propagation, holes are drilled at each end of a crack. The question is whether the cracks on the Bridge class were unusual and whether any of them could develop into brittle fracture – that is, literally a snapping force. The paper points out that it is probably impossible to estimate the fatigue life of a ship. This is because the 'material used in construction is far from uniform in quality and it is even possible that it will not all come from the same source'.[12]

Then there are problems in estimating the nature and speed of corrosion. More critical, as we shall see in the next chapter, is the issue of welding:

> The welding of a huge structure like a large bulk carrier is never perfect . . . That there will be defects is not seriously in doubt, but their distribution and seriousness is not something that can easily be assessed . . . Unfortunately the fatigue properties of the hull can be greatly affected by the quality and disposition of welds.[13]

Hull stresses are not limited to those brought about at sea. A ship's hull has unladen still water stresses too. Then again, detecting the beginning of cracks in a ship the size of these bulk carriers may be nearly impossible.

Finally there is the question whether or not the *Derbyshire* was constructed at Frame 65 in Grade A steel, which, as mentioned elsewhere, has a 'low notch' toughness or high brittle fracture propensity.

At the heart of the analysis lay the issue of ship *strength*. This is what the traditionalists have dwelt upon. Crudely, if the stresses at some point exceed a prescribed value the hull will fail. What the paper dealt with was fluctuating stresses which lead to cracking; and the concept that those cracks will grow. Thus by 'normal' standards the consideration of Frame 65 would not lead to any question of its strength *within the ship's whole girder*. The bending moment research by the BSRA showed the ship could sustain considerable forces. As the RINA paper says, this reveals nothing. The whole point is that ships are not rigid; masters of big bulkers will regularly tell of a twelve-foot flexing of their ships in a seaway, between bow and bridge:

> The hypothesis that we advanced is that repeated high stresses brought about by wave action caused the initiation of a crack (or cracks) which then spread and became sufficiently large as to endanger the ship. This prediction was made in the light of stress analysis and not based on any detailed consideration of crack initiation or crack propagation.[14]

Looking at what was known of the other ships, the paper concluded that all the evidence was available to suggest they were right. But, to back this conclusion further, they point to an unpublished paper by the BSRA, again using the traditional analysis, which had looked at cracking specifically and concluded 'the outcome of such a projection of events would have been massive hull failure at or about 65 frame station'.[15] In Part III we shall be looking at the *Derbyshire* formal inquiry of 1987 and 1988, which concluded there was unlikely to have been structural failure, and that Frame 65 was constructed properly, as was the ship.

In the next chapter we shall look at the way the Bridge class ships were built. This final piece of the jigsaw reveals the *Derbyshire* at her birth. Was she a jinxed ship, as some of her crew have alleged? Can it be fairly said that there was something wrong with her design in way of Frame 65? Is there evidence, not only of the problems she suffered during her working life, but from the testimony of those who built her, that in one way or another she was doomed?

10

How the Ships were Built

We have reached the heart of the matter after a long journey. We have come to Haverton Hill shipyard, on the Wear, Teesside. Once the pride of Britain, it is now a wasteland, a deserted, blasted heath of debris, old iron and rubbish.

Haverton Hill has been closed since 1980. Many of its workforce have never again found proper jobs and their skills, which built so many ships, have been lost. That they were skilled there is no doubt: but skill alone is not enough. The building of great ships demands good management, at all levels.

By the late 1960s when this part of the story begins, the shipbuilding system was creaking badly everywhere. There was too little investment and poor management; and the heavy-handed influence of trade unions helped to squeeze the British out of world shipping. The result was a desperate effort to save shipbuilding from Japan, and the Labour government was offering investment grants to anyone to build ships in Britain.

From the late 1960s Haverton Hill yard was owned by Swan Hunter, who had taken it over from Furness Shipbuilding Company, an independent yard which closed in mid-1968. Swan Hunter had a worldwide reputation for the ships they built. Their headquarters was at Wallsend, and so Haverton Hill yard was controlled by a local director responsible for day-to-day production. He was helped by departmental managers in charge of shop fabrication, ship erection, welding and what was known as NDT, non-destructive testing. Design, however, remained the responsibility of a technical director at Wallsend.

Building a ship is a complex operation. Time and technology have taken some of the burden away from the armies of shipbuilders who used to swarm over a building ship; none the less in the early 1970s Haverton Hill still employed over 200 welders.

These men were building each ship in prefabricated sections, a method of build which had originated in the Second World War, in the USA, and much like building a model in Lego: a lot of little bricks, each carefully numbered in the fabrication shops, had to be moved to the slip where they

Above: The last of the Bridge Class: the *Liverpool Bridge* (later renamed the *Derbyshire*).

Below: The *Derbyshire* at her last drydock in Sasebo, Japan (April 1980). The picture of her rudder and propeller gives some idea of the size of the ship.

Life aboard the *Derbyshire*.

Above left: The engine control room.

Above right: **Airlifting injured crew member** (1978). Note people standing on hatch cover. The hatch covers rolled open sideways from the centre line.

The engine room.

Loading tapioca pellets in Thailand in January 1978 (see p.47).

One of the only known pictures of the *Derbyshire*'s lifeboat as sighted by the *Taiei Maru* six weeks after the sinking.

Curly Baylis

Below left:
Cathie Musa

Below right:
Ronnie Musa

Above: Early stages in the construction of the *Furness Bridge* at the Haverton Hill yard, October 1969–January 1970.

Below: The launch of Ship number 25 – the *Furness Bridge* in 1971; the first of the Bridge class. At 926 feet long and 145 feet wide she was, at the time, the world's largest OBO carrier with the highest-powered diesel engine yet built in Britain.

Above: The construction of the fifth ship: *Sir Alexander Glen. Below:* The launch of the *Sir Alexander Glen* in 1975.

The sister ships.

Above: The *Tyne Bridge*. *Below:* The *Sir Alexander Glen*. *Bottom:* The *Furness Bridge*.

The *Kowloon Bridge* sinking. At this stage she was clearly sinking by the head, and the superstructure on the stern section is showing no signs of splitting at Frame 65; a point on the deck just ahead of the lifeboat.

Demands for an enquiry.

The *Kowloon Bridge* now split in two with the foremast rising above the sea.

Peter Ridyard.

Ridyard's models.

Above: Frame 65 can be seen marked on the model. *Below:* Viewed from above, showing area between No. 9 hold and the pumproom, divided by Frame/Bulkhead 65.

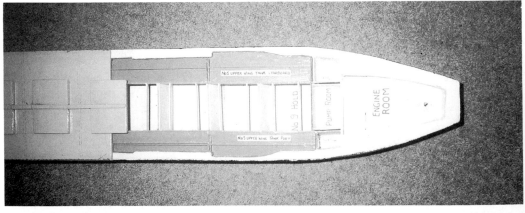

were welded into place. In the case of the Bridge class, thousands of pieces had to be assembled. There is nothing wrong with this method – it is now the way that thousands of ships are built.

Welded ships are very different from riveted ships. The old method of steel shipbuilding was to lay plates against each other with a row of holes punched in each plate. Hundreds of steel rivets were then banged through these holes at a high temperature and then hammered flat. The ships that were built like this were immensely strong, woven in steel. Of course the plates 'worked' and water might seep in. Ensuring the rivets were well and truly home was an art in which British shipbuilders excelled. If a plate was holed it was still held in place. Plates almost never fell off.

Welded ships, on the other hand, have suffered from a number of problems, one of which is corrosion in the weld itself. The chemistry of welds is another highly complex field, but in certain conditions welds can and do fail. Welded ships flex in different ways too. What is crucial is that every weld is good, and not just those of the 'shell' plates, for the whole structure of a welded ship is part of its integrity.

As we have seen, arguments over ship 'girder' strength have been frequently picked over. The quality of the build, for each of the Bridge class, has remained a vital part of the argument. Swan Hunter has maintained throughout that each of these ships was built to an exacting standard. The formal inquiry concluded that 'the *Derbyshire* was properly designed and properly built and that materials of the approved standards were used in her building'. The other side – the relatives, various experts including welding experts, and trade union officials – have harboured a suspicion that all was not well at Haverton Hill during the six years of the building of the Bridge class OBOs. This was supported by the testimony at the formal inquiry by those who were working there. Because this is at the very heart of the matter, we will present both cases as fully as space allows. Our own judgement is made at the end of this chapter.

The context of the building is significant. The OBO ships had emerged in the 1960s as an economic way of using a huge bulk or oil carrier interchangeably. The idea had emerged from Sweden in the Naess ships. Building an OBO was complicated, not least because the hatch covers have to be gas-tight for any oil or oil products. British shipbuilders had little knowledge of these ships prior to the Bridge class. But problems associated with these ships had been identified; these included:

high shear forces in the side shell structure caused by loading in alternate holds; large hull girder bending moments; *extremely high bending and shear loads in transverse bulkheads, especially in way of the lower stools, because of the absence of horizontal stringers* [our emphasis] . . . torsion of the upper wing tank structure, particularly in ships with long holds . . .[1]

The reason for building them, of course, was for the greatly expanded revenue capacity in a shipping market increasingly exercised by costs. All this had meant the evolution of the design in such a way that, unlike oil carriers, there were no longitudinal bulkheads. Instead a larger number of transverse bulkheads were used than was usual for pure ore carriers. 'The ore-carrying holds were often shorter than the empty holds and by stowing the ore in a small number of short holds full deadweight was achieved albeit with a high centre of gravity. Such ships offered the owner greater flexibility because a full deadweight of less dense cargoes such as coal or grain could also be carried, using all instead of alternate holds of the ship.'[2]

As the report points out, however, loading alternate holds generates high shear forces in the hull girder, for which reason special rules and classes were introduced by Lloyd's Register in 1964.

And as these were the largest ships ever to have been built in a British yard at that date and probably the largest bulk carriers being built anywhere in the world, they were intended to take part in the recovery of British shipbuilding in its struggle to escape its immediate past and come to terms with a very different shipping world. The container had made its first serious appearance, the Far East was proving how well, and cheaply, it could build big ships; furthermore in the late 1960s Britain still believed in her traditional industries – if they could only be helped to embrace what Prime Minister Harold Wilson had called 'the white heat of the technological revolution'. In these traditional industries, however, trade unions were still able to flex enormously powerful muscles against revolutionary working practices of which they did not approve.

It is clear that the formal inquiry of 1987 did not address these wider issues, concentrating only on the immediate question of how the ships were built. Yet the climate in which they were built was crucial too. In brief, they were an experimental design, and as William Jowett, a Fabrication Manager, said at the formal inquiry, 'We knew we were going to have problems just by the sheer nature of the size of the ship and this was why quality control was so important.'[3]

Ship number 25 was to become the *Furness Bridge*. She was built on the slip, that is, on the sloping base from which she would be launched. The alternative is to build a ship in a graving dock, flood the dock and float the ship out, which is a gentler way. Building a ship in thousands of sections on a slope poses one obvious problem, that of the alignment of each section, as the calculations that have to be made must take into account the angle of the slope (assuming, over a thousand feet and more, it is a constant angle). There were eight shipbuilders called to the formal inquiry: William Jowett and Gerald Leak, Fabrication Managers; Archy Miller, Berth Manager; George Hodgson, Head Welding Supervisor; Donald Ellis, Production Manager; George Parnaby, Head Foreman Burner; David Spendley, a draughtsman; and finally, and late in the day, Douglas Mallam, a welder.

There were comments about the pressure the yard had been under for ship number 25, from George Hodgson, for example:

I recall that with the *Furness Bridge* the yard was under a great deal of pressure following the reopening to comply with the various instalment dates and key dates for which the vessel had been programmed. In my position as Head Supervisor the procedure in the fabrication shops was that all steel units were to be dry surveyed before erection on to the vessel . . . However on this vessel the pressures on us to get the steel units out of the fabrication shops meant that in the majority of cases I do not believe we had time to survey the units . . . This meant it had to be surveyed totally on the building berth, which meant a much more difficult exercise since staging and lighting are much better organised in the shops in comparison to the building berths . . .[4]

Douglas Mallam suggested that there was bad practice but the formal inquiry dismissed his testimony. He had alleged that while he had been working on the *Derbyshire* on an unstiffened shell plate situated on the port side aft just above the waterline and abaft the Engine Control Room, he discovered that the plate was badly laminated (splitting). The formal inquiry stated: 'he reported this to his supervisors but claimed that he was instructed to complete the work without removing the plate.' The formal inquiry concluded 'considerable doubt must exist concerning the credibility of his uncorroborated, sometimes confused and generally unreliable evidence' and thought that even if true, the result would not have affected the ship.

These comments were isolated evidence at the formal inquiry. The overall impression given by the shipbuilding witnesses, with one or two caveats, was that the ships of the *Derbyshire* class were built to a very high standard with immense care being taken over the welding and the quality controls at all stages.

From the weight of this evidence, the formal inquiry concluded:

The *Derbyshire* was designed to have ample reserves of hull girder strength even if the particular girder connection at Frame 65 did not conform to an ideal theoretical design practice. Evidence presented supported the view that the ship was built in accordance with the drawings and specifications.

It appears most likely that the doublers on the sister ships were introduced during post-construction repairs. It is very unlikely, therefore, that any would have been fitted on the *Derbyshire* during initial construction. No evidence was given of structural misalignment on the *Derbyshire*.

Subsequent evidence was heard that the reserves of hull girder strength were such that even if some structural misalignment had existed and was equivalent to a complete disconnection at the Frame 65/engine room bulkhead cruciform, the overall hull girder strength would not have been seriously affected.[5]

Yet the ship did sink. What of the design, and the way it was changed?

The initial design work for these ships, including the class submissions (for Lloyd's Register) was done at the Wallsend office but the steel working drawings for the hull including structural modifications were prepared by the local office at Haverton Hill. Thus the design office at Wallsend was responsible for the design calculations, the main drawings and for deciding what tank tests ought to be carried out (for working out the engine size). Lloyd's Register, in any normal circumstances, does not design ships; but they ask for amendments where they consider it necessary, and they approve the drawings submitted to them. These have to conform to the ship's class rules, in this case applicable to both tankers and dry cargo ships, since there were then no separate rules for OBOs. Working drawings are produced out of the master plans and these too have to be seen and approved by Lloyd's surveyors. Once these are approved they are used in the production of the parts for the ships. Lloyd's surveyors were continuously on site checking the way the ships were being built, as was the owner's representative.

Of course, at the start, the plans that were being worked to included longitudinals which went through the 65 bulkhead or frame. But an International Maritime Organisation requirement in OBOs was that the aft hold (number nine) had to be separated from the pump room wing tanks (in case there were leaks when the ships carried liquid cargoes). This meant the addition of cofferdams at Frame 64. When this happened the problem of access to these arose and a decision was taken to terminate the longitudinal girders ahead of bulkhead 65 and to continue them on the other side (with alignment).

The formal inquiry said this:

To maintain the structural strength of the ship in this region it is necessary to ensure that there is suitable integration or scarphing of the structural components. This is achieved either:

(i) by ensuring that the principal longitudinal structural members such as the deck, deck longitudinals and girders are carried through the transition area; or

(ii) if it is necessary to terminate longitudinal components, to make certain that arrangements are such that their load carrying characteristics are continued through the structure without giving rise to abrupt changes in sectional area and the associated stress concentrations which may lead to the development of fatigue fractures.[6]

In the *Derbyshire*, the report goes on, the internal members were stopped on the forward side of the bulkhead at Frame 65. As they say, the question is then whether the required continuity was achieved.

The evidence gathered by Peter Ridyard, and obtained during the investigations of the Department of Transport about misalignment in the other ships, indicates it was not, and this we will return to below. There is the other question of who approved the change in the first design, and why no plans of it can apparently be found. We note, of course, that Lloyd's Register has said that it would have considered the change to have still kept the ships in class.

The ships were built in sections of about 70 tons, this size being determined by the equipment the yard had and the lifting capacity of the cranes, and the tractors. Big units can distort; small ones imply many more welds. The formal inquiry report merely notes the construction but points out that for 'speed of construction as well as for the benefits to be derived from down-hand welding', some units were built upside down. These units were then put together and checks were made for alignment (which was checked by Lloyd's surveyors). The Lloyd's surveyor in charge at Haverton Hill was Sid Turpie. At the formal inquiry his methods were discussed. Turpie used a hammer. He used to strike a bulkhead plate on one side with this hammer and, depending on the sound (dull or echoing), he was convinced he was able to pick up the exact position in which the material on the other side was abutting against the bulkhead. Turpie is now dead but in a statement he said: 'Alignment was generally achieved by visual inspection but where "blind" by hammer testing and checking welding marks.' He admitted that where thick plating was involved this was difficult, 'if not impossible and [here] accuracy of unit preparation carried out by shipyard would have to be relied upon'. The formal inquiry report concluded that 'alignment of longitudinals in way of Frame 65 was particularly difficult to ascertain on the partially-constructed ship'.

This has to be set in context. As we have said, these ships were enormous structures and as the sections were being handled on the berth, assembled and welded together, so the opportunity for close inspection receded, not least because in many cases the act of welding sections together prevented access to some of the surfaces. As well as this, there are immense problems associated with detecting not just misalignment but also whether the welds are completely satisfactory. To assume every weld on a giant ship is perfect would be stretching credulity; however, it is the integrity of the design and the building taken overall which is responsible for structural strength and which may, in the end, be said to be more critical than anything else.

The checks over the quality of the building were continuous and they were not just being made by Swan Hunter. The inquiry found:

A senior representative of Bibby Line, the owners of the *Derbyshire*, supervised all or some of the construction of four ships of the class . . . excluding the *Derbyshire*. Whilst somewhat critical of the standards and practices used in the shipyard he asserted that he was never obliged to accept sub-standard workmanship in any critical area. He stated that the degree of misalignment subsequently reported in the first five ships could not possibly have been due to faults in the original construction.[7]

The report went on to say that another owner's representative was critical of the welding procedures and the activities of the quality control department for the first ship but considered that things had got better (the *Derbyshire* was the last to be built).

We will never know whether there were plans of the changes to the longitudinal arrangements in the ships after *Furness Bridge*. The Wallsend office say they never saw the cofferdam design. We know that it was made by the design firm of Spendley, Richardson and Helm and that no naval architect was involved. Did any of the local Lloyd's surveyors see this other change? Apparently not, for had they seen it they would have submitted it to their head office for approval.

The alternative, that the plans were made, submitted and then lost or destroyed is, in our opinion, to be ruled out by the improbability of five sets of plans at Wallsend and in Lloyd's Register in London all going missing. There was, though, a bigger question of design. Although the formal inquiry did not say so directly, presentation of the evidence suggests that everyone could at least be happy over the concept and the execution of the plans: the basic design was sound.

But one man did not agree.

At the formal inquiry a Swedish ship designer, Leif Andersson was called. He worked for Kockums, in their hull design department. The original OBO type, the so-called Naess ships, were designed and built by Eriksberg in Gothenburg, Sweden. Their size was restricted by the shipyard building ways and by the width of the river into which they were launched. The much larger ships of the size of the Bridge series were designed and built by Kockums in Malmö. Andersson was asked about the original design, ship number 25:

> I have considered the original design of the *Furness Bridge* in the area of the bulkhead at Frame 65 where the longitudinal hatch side girder meets the bulkhead. In principle, subject to what I say below, I consider it a good design. However the hatch side girder should meet for a greater distance aft of Frame 65, four to five metres would be about the right distance. Additionally, as the longitudinal is 29mm thick forward of the bulkhead, it should be continued aft of the bulkhead at the same thickness before being reduced in stages . . . it is important to have the same thickness of plate on both sides of the bulkhead to take care of stress forces. Secondly, special care has to be taken with the welding.[8]

Andersson said he thought that Lloyd's rules on welding were fairly basic and not sufficient for modern ships. He was later questioned by the Lloyd's Counsel at the inquiry and became confused, as we shall see in Chapter 11. Andersson's point was that perhaps all classification societies needed to look more closely at their rules on this and other matters. The classification society rules did not really matter when ships were built well above standard – as most were in Europe before the economic crisis began in shipping.

Andersson also pointed out that whatever the design of the Bridge OBOs as originally approved, alignment of the parts of the ship would have been vital. But in any case when he came to see how the design had been altered, he could not believe his eyes: 'The design alterations would not have been acceptable in a Swedish shipbuilding yard. I am surprised that the modification was apparently approved by Lloyd's.' However, we know that it was not approved, because they have not got the plans, unless possibly at local level.

On the matter of alignment there remains a huge dispute. Yard witnesses maintained that it was not a problem. They were backed up by the surveyors called to the formal inquiry, who all said that they had checked alignments carefully, and that if doublers and fillers had been fitted they would have seen them and would have ordered their removal.

As William Jowett, one of the Fabrication Managers said: 'we knew we were going to have problems just by the sheer nature of the size of the ship and this was why quality control was so important'.

On quality control the formal inquiry concluded:

The standards to which the quality control personnel worked were contained in a 'Standards Book' printed and circulated to all quality control and production staff. The standards were initially derived from experiences gained in the building of large ships at Haverton Hill but were finally replaced by the wider experience of Swan Hunter. They described in detail the limits of acceptability if actual construction differed from the drawings. These standards had not been formally approved by Lloyd's Register of Shipping but the contents of the Standards Book and its use in the shipyard were known to the resident Lloyd's Register surveyors.[9]

On the issue of the question of misalignment the inquiry decided:

Although examples of misalignment in ships of the class, other than the *Derbyshire*, had been reported at various times by Lloyd's surveyors and others, the personnel of Swan Hunter were adamant that misalignments of the magnitude subsequently found on these other ships would not have been permitted by their management or overseeing authorities during the building process.

In their opinion, such misalignment must have been introduced in the course of "in-service" repair activities. In particular, the fitting and welding of pads, liners, fillings or filler plates other than in exceptionally allowed circumstances in structurally non-critical areas of the ship could not, it was claimed, have been carried out in the building yard. It was acknowledged that minor misalignments or the cranking of free material in order to achieve satisfactory structural alignment did occur with managerial and quality control approval but certainly not on a regular basis or in structurally sensitive areas. *Our conclusion is* that there was no evidence supporting either misalignment or the fitting of doublers or liners in the *Derbyshire*.[10]

The issue of doublers and pads is vital. Peter Ridyard, among others, found doublers fitted at Frame 65: these were variously called at the inquiry – which led to some confusion – but, basically, they are sections of steel inserted between the longitudinal girders and the bulkhead (in this case, number 65). With reference to the *Tyne Bridge*, the doublers found were later proved to have been fitted at a German yard. Peter Ridyard's feeling subsequently was that all doublers were fitted after the vessels went into service (as the inquiry believed). The fact that doublers were found in each subsequent ship following the *Furness Bridge* would suggest that misalignment was already present. This would result in weld fractures where the girders were secured to the bulkhead. To repair these defects, the girders would be cut back sufficiently to slot in a doubler plate, thus ensuring that the stress in the area was being spread over the plate rather than being concentrated at a point (a 'hard spot').

Both the owners of the ships and Lloyd's Register have to know when and why these doublers were fitted.

On the issue of misalignment we have plenty of evidence. Again we turn to the RINA paper of Bishop, Price and Temarel, which succinctly draws it together, and we are grateful for their permission to quote extensively from it:

Layout

To explain the nature of this problem it will help if we first briefly explain the layout of the ship in the vicinity of Frame 65 in a rough and ready way. In Fig. 1 we are, so to speak, looking into the hull from above with the deck removed. The figure shows Frame 65 with a transverse bulkhead forming the after wall of no. 9 hold. No. 9 hold is separated from no. 8 hold by other transverse bulkheads at Frame 95. The forward wall of no. 8 hold is a bulkhead at Frame 125. Water ballast may be carried in the no. 5 upper wing tanks on the port and starboard sides; these tanks extend forward from bulkhead 65 to bulkhead 125. The vertical inboard sides of the wing tanks are longitudinal bulkheads that serve as main strength members. The hatches sit on these longitudinals.

Frame 65 marks the end of the nine holds and hence the point at which there is a change in the structural configuration. Two longitudinal bulkheads abut against the after face of the transverse bulkhead at Frame 65 in line with the pair of longitudinal strength members, as indicated in Fig. 2.

The two longitudinal members forward of bulkhead 65 play a major

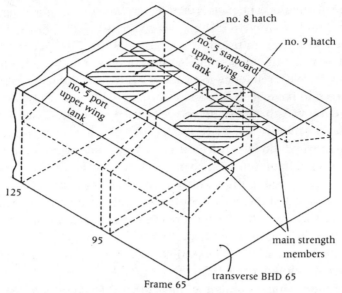

Fig. 1 Simplified internal arrangement forward of Frame 65, showing holds 8 and 9 and the no. 5 upper wing ballast tanks. The main strength members are 35'6" from the centre line of the hull, form the inboard longitudinal bulkheads of the upper wing tanks and are of grade A steel. These members are referred to as 'girders' and their cross section is 800mm × 29mm.

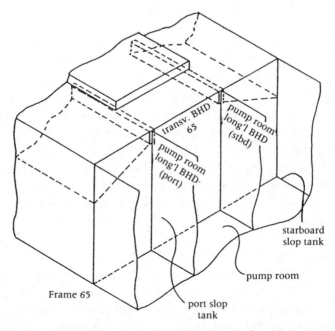

Fig. 2 Simplified arrangement immediately abaft Frame 65, showing the port and starboard slop tanks and the pump room separated by longitudinal bulkheads 35'6" from the ship centre line. Cofferdams are not shown.

part in the symmetric flexural strength of the hull and they raise an important question of design. Should they be continued through bulkhead 65 or should they be terminated on one side of that bulkhead as shown in Fig. 2? If the latter course is adopted, particular care must be taken to weld the structural components accurately so as to preserve continuity and so maintain the structural strength of the hull. With the arrangement shown in Fig. 2 it is necessary that there be proper alignment between the members on each side of the transverse bulkhead and that the welding is of high quality.

It was originally intended that the upper wing tanks should extend 450mm aft of Frame 65, and [evidence] suggests that this was so with *Furness Bridge*. Fig. 3 shows the approved method of construction. The

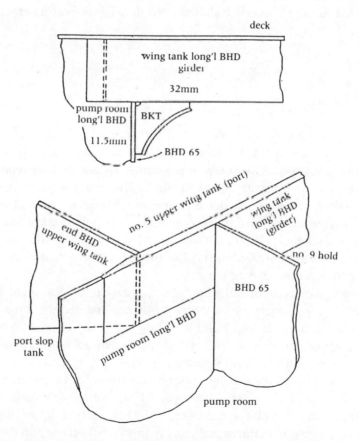

Fig. 3 The approved method of construction. The upper wing tanks extended aft of Frame 65 and the girder passes through transverse bulkhead 65. This arrangement was unsatisfactory as the slop tank was separated from no. 9 hold by bulkhead 65 only (below the wing tank), raising the possibility of dry cargo contamination.

longitudinal strength member (which serves as the inboard longitudinal bulkhead of the no. 5 upper wing tank as we have seen) passes through transverse bulkhead no. 65. At a point aft of Frame 65, this member is tapered and then butt welded to the longitudinal bulkhead in the pump room. It will be noted that a flanged supporting bracket is incorporated in the design.

The approved method of construction was modified in most ships of this class in circumstances that have not been fully explained. The motivation for this change was at least in part the wish to isolate the slop tanks from no. 9 hold and from the pump room by coffer dams. The upper wing tank and its longitudinal bulkhead (i.e. the 'strength member') did not pass through transverse bulkhead 65 but were terminated forward of it. Like the longitudinal bulkhead in the pump room it was welded to the transverse bulkhead. No flanged supporting bracket was used.

Misalignment

As Fig. 3 suggests, the approved design of the ship was such that the inboard surface of the wing tank longitudinal bulkhead is coplanar with the inboard surface of the pump room longitudinal bulkhead. (Both were 35 ft 6 in from the ship centre line.) The layout sketched in Fig. 4 is not strictly correct in this detail, therefore, as it shows the mid planes of the two bulkheads lined up (as one might expect from considerations of structural theory) rather than the two inboard surfaces. Misalignment of the two longitudinal bulkheads has therefore to be measured by reference to coplanar inboard surfaces.

Perhaps on account of the modular approach to fabrication of the hull, significant misalignment of the two longitudinal members was found. This is illustrated in Fig. 5 and it is shown that the effect is to impart a fluctuating distortion to the transverse bulkhead 65. This would be associated with high local stresses.

The amount of the misalignment varied from ship to ship in the class, and estimates of its magnitude vary from source to source. Typical estimates are indicated in the table. It will be seen that the misalignment in *Derbyshire* is not known and (surprisingly) that on the port side of the *Kowloon Bridge* is also unknown. There is disagreement in the available documentation as to the amount of misalignment, and its variation from the top of the girder to the bottom.

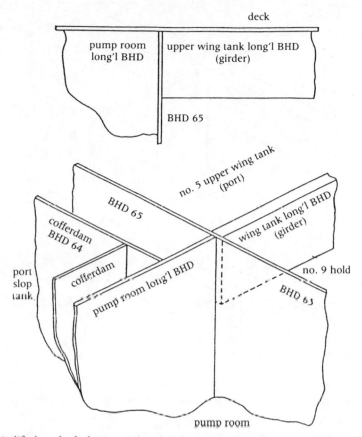

Fig. 4 Modified method of construction showing how cofferdams were introduced.

It will be noticed that 'filler plates' (or 'doublers') are shown on one side of transverse bulkhead 65 or the other in most ships. When, and by whom, these doublers were installed appears to be something of a mystery. Nor is it clear why the arrangement shown in Fig. 4 was adopted, since cofferdams could presumably have been installed as shown in Fig. 6 without terminating the strength member at Frame 65.

The significance of the misalignment is a matter of debate. The conclusion that has to be drawn . . . is that it could constitute the source of fatigue cracks by reason of high local stresses and that those cracks could well propagate. The 'traditional' view, quoting a classification society (Lloyd's Register of Shipping) is that 'any misalignment of the inboard vertical side of the topside tank with the pump room longitudinal bulkhead at transverse bulkhead 65 is significant only for local strength aspects'. This disagreement is really quite central.[11]

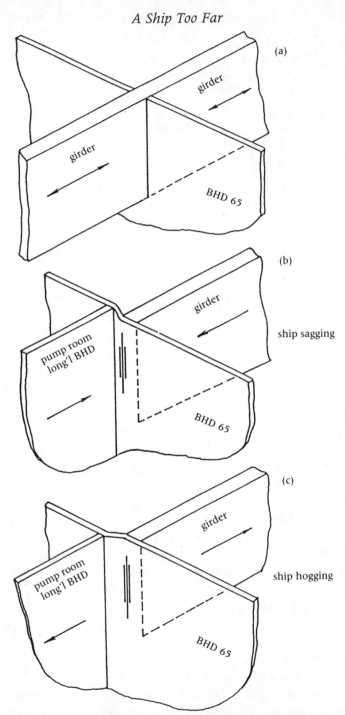

Fig. 5 The effects of hull sagging and hogging. When the girder passes through bulkhead 65 as in (a), no distortion of that bulkhead occurs. When the pump room longitudinal bulkhead is not in line with the girder, as in (b) and (c), distortion does occur.

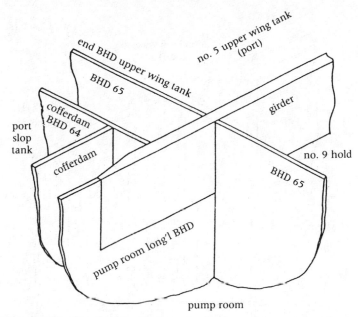

Fig. 6 Demonstration that the introduction of cofferdams did not make it necessary to terminate the girder at transverse bulkhead 65.

The Tyne Bridge modification

Another arrangement, of which a simplified sketch is shown in Fig. 7, was adopted by way of repair after the shortcomings of the layout in Fig. 4 had been recognised. The strength member was cropped back and then extended by a thicker and tougher steel plate passed through bulkhead 65 which was reinforced. The supporting bracket was now embodied in the extension. (In addition, areas of the deck adjacent to the after corners of no. 9 hold were cut out and replaced with thicker plate of higher grade steel.)

The formal inquiry concluded the following:

Our conclusion is that the *Derbyshire* was properly designed and properly built and that materials of the approved standard were used in her building. We have carefully considered the evidence of fatigue cracking in the sister ships of the *Derbyshire* but we are not satisfied that the same factors were present in the *Derbyshire*, which may have led to fatigue cracking in the sister ships. Although damage has been sustained in the

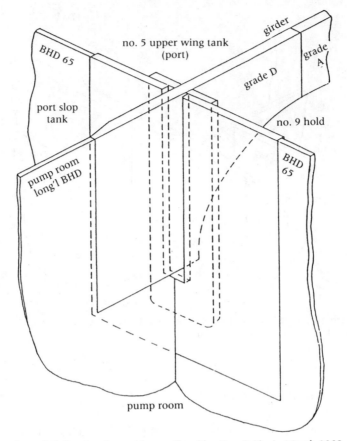

Fig. 7 Repair made following the accident suffered by *Tyne Bridge* in March 1982.

sister ships and one of them has been lost, the circumstances in which those events occurred were quite different to the circumstances of the *Derbyshire*, so far as they can be proved. It is to be noted that none of the sister ships has been lost as a direct consequence of fatigue cracking nor, in the one case where brittle fracture occurred, as a result of brittle fracture.[12]

opposite Table Misalignment of longitudinal bulkheads at Frame 65

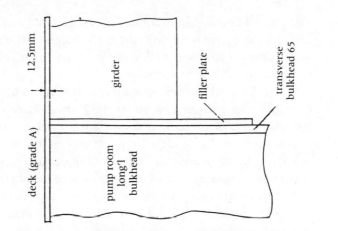

deck (grade A)

12.5mm

girder

filler plate

transverse
bulkhead 65

pump room
long'l
bulkhead

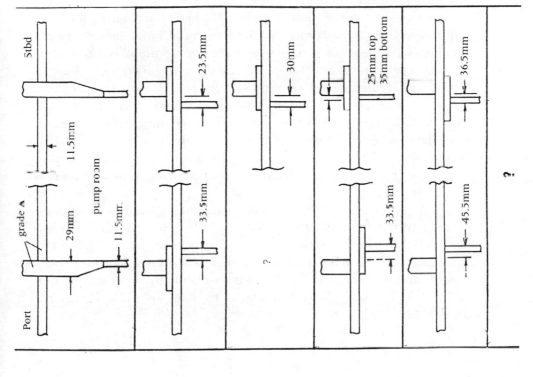

Stbd

11.5mm

grade A

pump room

29mm

11.5mm

Port

Furness Bridge

23.5mm

33.5mm

Tyne Bridge

30mm

?

Kowloon Bridge

25mm top
35mm bottom

33.5mm

Sir John Hunter

36.5mm

45.5mm

Sir Alexander Glen

?

Derbyshire

The reader in a case like this must, inevitably, make up her or his own mind about the story we have presented. The biggest stumbling block is the lack of a 'corpse'. It seems that all that the parties agree on is that the *Derbyshire* did sink, and that lives were lost.

We believe that the evidence for massive and sudden structural failure is overwhelming, not just based on the Bishop, Price and partners 'theory' but on what BSRA found, under certain conditions, and on the most likely explanation for the sudden disappearance of this huge ship.

Those who have argued for other explanations have of course relied on the circumstantial nature of the case for structural failure. We believe this tack is specious. We have the evidence from the other ships: they all had problems in the area of Frame/bulkhead 65. *Kowloon Bridge* split at this point when she sank – why?

We know that five of these ships had a different arrangement of the longitudinals. We cannot prove that this was crucial, but we believe it was. Common sense needs to intrude here, aside from technical issues.

If this was a conventional story, we would have ended there. Having examined all evidence available to us we believe the Frame 65 explanation for the loss of the *Derbyshire* is overwhelming. But this is not a conventional story. So far, it does not have an end. Two notable things have happened since she sank. First, the relatives will not give up. Second, recently it has become apparent that what happened to the *Derbyshire* may be a general problem for bulkers – and oil tankers. These two issues came together in the course of 1991.

First though, it seemed that there was a last chance to get to the bottom of all this, when the *Kowloon Bridge* loss resulted in a formal inquiry. Hopes among the relatives were raised as they had never been before. They were to be utterly dashed in the course of the months of the inquiry. One reason was the announcement made almost immediately by Treasury Counsel that the inquiry was unlikely to find the cause of the loss of MV *Derbyshire*.

Part III

Shockwaves

11

The Formal Inquiry: pains and painstaking

In 1987 it was announced there was going to be a formal inquiry into the loss of the *Derbyshire*. The sinking of the *Kowloon Bridge* had been the final link in the long-drawn-out chain of events between the sinking of the *Derbyshire*, Peter Ridyard's work, the research by BSRA and Bishop, Price and partners, and the endless work put in by Department of Transport officials: interviewing, travelling, pondering, analysing, theorising.

The inquiry opened on Monday, October 5th, in the Convocation Hall at Church House, Westminster. It was to be presided over by a Wreck Commissioner, Gerald Darling, and three assessors, Dr Baxter, Mr Bunnis and Captain Murray. In all, it was to call thirty-six witnesses and to receive written submissions from a further thirty-nine. The whole event lasted nearly five months (with a nine week break in the middle). It was, by any standards, a major affair.

The parties were represented by a posse of barristers: for the Department of Transport, for the owners, for Swan Hunter, for Lloyd's, and for fifteen of the relatives. The public was admitted – many people came from *Derbyshire* families and were to find the experience devastating.

The inquiry had been set a single question to answer: What caused the loss of the *Derbyshire*? In order to do that, three theories had to be considered, one of which concerned the structural strength of the *Derbyshire* in way of Frame 65. The original preamble by the Secretary of State said the *Derbyshire* had 'capsized', and the reason for that capsize was the issue. Immediately the Wreck Commissioner, Gerald Darling, had this word deleted, arguing that how she sank was a question still to be answered.

The opening speech, by Mr Steel for the Department of Transport, had seemed, to the relatives, to be 'on target'. In what follows we have quoted extensively from the forty-six volumes of transcripts, one for each day. This tells far more than the final report, simply by giving the verbatim comments of witnesses.

Steel opened on the Monday, after preliminary issues had been settled over vital questions such as when lunch would be taken. Relatives of the crew were to find throughout that the 'legal' way of doing business was distressing: one remarked that it was all in-jokes and chumminess. Steel began:

Large she may have been but there was no apparent reason for her connections to lack complete confidence in her . . . So, not surprisingly, her fate was not just a matter of acute distress for the dependants of those on board but the cause of considerable disquiet in the industry at large.

But, he ended, 'it may still be that no firm conclusions can be drawn'.

Steel had wanted the inquiry, which was conducting its own researches, to look at the Department of Transport report of March 1986 (which we discussed in Chapter 6): 'I think it might be helpful to the Tribunal to see that March 1986 report which was published . . . Sir, you will find . . . '

The Commissioner instantly interrupted: 'It is not usual to look at other reports, is it necessary?'

Steel argued strongly that the court should look at the report ('it is very much a public document') and the Commissioner asked if other Counsel objected.

Brice, for the relatives interposed: 'No, I have no objection . . . May I mention [that] for you to see only that report would be incomplete because it is only the second half of what was a major report which was begun in July 1985.'

Steel: 'It would be best, at this stage, to stick with the March 1986 report.'

Commissioner: 'If these are reports on the same questions as we are considering it is not customary to *waste time* [our emphasis] looking at them . . . '

Steel: 'I think it is not a waste of time.'

Hamilton (Lloyd's Counsel): We have no objection . . . '

Commissioner: 'I would prefer not to have my mind clouded by other people's reports.'

This argument was fundamental. Steel wanted the inquiry to look at the final report, in which there had been many alterations; Brice wanted the inquiry to look at both. In either case the Bishop, Price and partners work would have been discussed. The argument continued, therefore, with Steel actually trying to read the final report into his opening submission. The Commissioner interjected.

Commissioner: 'Who were the authors of this? This looks as though *it goes to the very questions we are supposed to be deciding* [our emphasis] . . . Why is it relevant, what has happened since 1980 other than clearing the yardarm of the Department of Transport . . . We shall not be relying on this Report . . . '

Steel: 'I am anxious to assist the Court in any way it wants, if it is not of assistance I will not read it. I gather other parties thought that it would be helpful . . . May I invite you to close that document and I will simply say this, that following the original decision not to hold a public inquiry the two consultants were invited to carry out some work assessing the strength of the ship and her design at the same time primarily through the work of Mr Ridyard who was the father of one of the officers on board the *Derbyshire* . . . The next stage was that in late 1986, after another of the sister ships, the *Kowloon Bridge*, sustained a casualty in heavy weather . . . as a result of preliminary investigation of the Hong Kong government (where she had been registered) it was decided . . . to hold a formal inquiry into the loss of the *Derbyshire because it was thought that certain items of damage sustained by the Kowloon Bridge might be material to the loss of the Derbyshire'* (our emphasis).

Steel continued very much in the same vein, to push the issue of the way the *Derbyshire* had been built. He pointed out the significance of the sister ships and their history: 'The first vessel of the series, *World Pathfinder* [formerly *Furness Bridge*] was built so that the longitudinal members situated 35 feet 6 inches off the centreline, port and starboard, forward of Frame 65 (which were also the upper wing tank side plates) passed through the transverse bulkhead at Frame 65 and continued aft for approximately 450mm until they met longitudinal members situated in the vessel's pump room. The remaining five ships were built so that the wing tanks, together with the port and starboard longitudinal members, terminated at the forward side of the transverse bulkhead at Frame 65. Longitudinal members then continued, as separate sections, aft of Frame 65. This modification was approved by Lloyd's Register of London'.

Apart from the last statement, which we believe now was never the case, all this was an exact and precise record of the ship's design. Steel went on: 'It was decided to add a cofferdam between the slop tanks and the cargo hold on each side . . . That was necessary if one was going to carry any cargo in number nine hold and slops in the slop tank.' He said that it had been owing to the problems of access to this area, after the cofferdams had been added, that the longitudinals had been terminated forward of Frame 65.

He went on: 'To add to the confusion, and confusion in the past has been occasioned by it, it is clear that this change in construction design was approved by Lloyd's but the confusion reined [sic] because if one goes back to . . . the plans for the series, despite the change in construction, still showed the hatchside girder scarphed into the longitud-inal bulkhead. . . .'

He went into great detail about the problems in each ship in the region of Frame 65, ending with a graphic and precise account of the demise of the *Kowloon Bridge*. Steel's discussion of Frame 65 takes up fifteen pages of single-spaced transcript. At the end he mentions that there may be other reasons for the *Derbyshire's* loss.

There followed readings from parts of the various research reports. Steel read from the BSRA research but not the Bishop, Price and partners work. He went on to read from a study by Burness and Corlett, done for Swan Hunter, which said the ship had suffered progressive hatch cover failure. This same research said that 'no conclusions on the possible cause of loss can be drawn from the reported damage to the lifeboat'.

Finally, however, Steel got in a reference to the Bishop, Price and partners work.

Instantly Mr Hamilton, one of Lloyd's Counsels, was on his feet: 'That is the report in respect of which we enquired whether it was to be relied on by the Department. We were told that it was not so.'

Steel then asked if parties wished this report to go in.

Commissioner: 'Until such representations are made you will be careful not to rely upon or mention the Bishop, Price report.'

Steel, struggling now, pointed out that he could hardly avoid mention-ing it as it was in the report made by John Jubb, a welding expert to be called by the relatives.

Commissioner: 'Once objection has fairly and squarely been made there is no question of putting in that report, as it were, by a side wind; *it ceases to exist*' [our emphasis].

Professor Bishop was not called to the formal inquiry and the research was never explored. Frame 65 did get much more attention, though not all of it was friendly. The final report concluded: 'The combination of circum-stances necessary to postulate separation of the hull at Frame No. 65 is very unlikely, though some element of doubt must remain.'

Mr Brice, acting for the relatives, had been stating earlier in the inquiry the case for massive failure at Frame 65 as a cause well worth investigating.

Commissioner: 'What are your reasons for saying that? . . . One further question, why did none of the other ships get lost by having the after part falling off . . . None of the others was lost in this way, yet there is evidence that so far as these cracks in way of Frame 65 *are material at all* [our emphasis] the other ships had rather more cracks than the *Derbyshire* ever had . . .'

On Day 45, five months later, the following exchange took place between the Wreck Commissioner and Brice, now making his closing speech.

Commissioner: 'The *Derbyshire* was built to the modified result?'

Brice: 'The *Derbyshire* was built to the modified design, as modified after ship 25 (*Furness Bridge*) but not modified as were three of these ships in 1982 for the simple reason that she was lost in 1980.'

Commissioner: 'These are modifications which took place after one of the other ships suffered some damage?'

Brice: 'Yes, sir.'

Commissioner: 'Several ships in the class were modified?'

Brice? 'Yes, sir.'

Commissioner: 'Several are still sailing the seas. It is not a *class* [our emphasis] of dud ships that sank?'

Brice: 'I do not think I have ever suggested that . . . '

It was subsequent to this exchange, which makes us wonder whether the Wreck Commissioner had grasped one of the central points about the ships, that he and his assessors went to see the *Sir Alexander Glen*, one of those remodified ships. Perhaps confusion arose because of the problem between understanding the first modifications (cutting off the continuous girders) and the *re*modifications, when some attempt was made to return to the *Furness Bridge* design.

Confusion over terminology dogged the inquiry throughout. The way in which feet and inches became millimetres and metres hardly helped. Neither did an understanding of what 'doublers' were and whether they were the same as 'pads'. The technicalities of welding, shipbuilding in sections and quality controls were not helped either by the paucity of good photographs showing details of the building.

The inquiry, it can fairly be said, was overwhelmed by paper, much of it highly technical. At the same time some paper was being given more weight than other. And we remain curious that while the inquiry looked at the *Sir Alexander Glen*, it did not look at the remains of the *Kowloon Bridge* which were brought to the Court, or any material or video from it. Yet the *Kowloon Bridge* had been the primary cause of their sitting in the first place, and was closest to the design of the *Derbyshire*, that is not remodified.

The proceedings dragged on. Finally on Tuesday, October 20th, Peter Ridyard was in the room. His testimony was read out, largely his curriculum vitae.

Commissioner: 'I do not think he can help us much, can he?'

And that was that. None of the Counsels, including Brice, asked Ridyard any questions at all. Relatives in the room gasped in disbelief.

After Ridyard came a succession of technical witnesses: four days on the nature of iron ore as a cargo and whether it could have shifted or 'liquefied'; two days on the weather and then an immense amount of testimony and cross-questioning about the hatch covers and whether 'progressive failure' was possible. That took four more days.

By then the inquiry had slipped into December. One witness was now recalled. This was Leif Andersson, whom we have met before (in Chapter 10). Andersson had made a number of points about the design of the area of Frame 65. Andersson was Swedish. His English was good but he was dealing with a highly technical subject. Lloyd's Counsel appears to have used the discrepancy between his ability to speak and follow English and Andersson's need to explain the technical details, to suggest that he did not always follow the argument. (This was not a courtroom, but one point made by a relative who attended was how insane it was to try to establish the truth of the *Derbyshire* loss in this adversarial way, where 'witnesses' were challenged as if they were guilty of some crime.)

Hamilton (for Lloyd's): 'Going back to the first of the necessary conditions for your theory of breaking apart at Frame 65, an existing crack in the deck when the ship entered Typhoon Orchid, in the *Derbyshire*, is to postulate that the crack was not seen by any member of the crew, is it not?'

Andersson: 'No, I do not think that is . . . '

Hamilton: 'That is right though, is it not? It postulates it was not seen by any member of the crew?'

Andersson: 'No, I do not think it postulates it has not been seen.'

Hamilton: 'You think they may have seen it and ignored it, do you?'

Andersson: 'In my mind that is not impossible, no.'

Hamilton: 'The officers and crew of a line of the reputation of Bibbys, they ignore cracks on the deck?'

Andersson: 'I did not say they ignore, I say I do not look upon it as a definite must that the crack has not been seen. Cracks are very often difficult to discover . . . The fact that cracks have occurred earlier to my mind says they can occur once more and very rapidly, that is my experience . . . '

But Andersson was doomed. Later, he had to admit some of his calculations had been wrong, not that they materially affected his conclusions. But it was the additional weapon the inquiry sought.

Commissioner: 'Mr Andersson, I think the time has come where it would be rather more helpful if you answered the questions yes or no when you can rather than making speeches. We are all very well aware you have a lot to say on these things.'

This remark has to be put in some context, compared, for example, with Dr Corlett's four-day disquisition on hatch covers or even Dr

Skinner's evidence on iron ore concentrates which took up three days.

By December, when a nine-week adjournment ensued, the Frame 65 'theory' was now the subject for a continuous attack by Counsels for Swan Hunter and Lloyd's.

Next, John Jubb, a welding expert, was called by Brice for the relatives. Unfortunately his testimony was split into two by the long adjournment. Jubb's examination was the last chance to reopen the question of how the ships were built.

He said: 'The history of this group of ships is a record of cracks, mis-alignments and doubler plates in the region of Frame 65, implying high local stresses in service . . . it is impossible to have confidence in a welded ship structure prone to fatigue cracking and local brittle fracture in material with no proven fracture toughness . . . This lack of confidence stemming from sub-standard welded details [which he had examined] in sister ships occurring during construction or repair, leads to the conclusion that the *Derbyshire's* hull was vulnerable to failure in the region of Frame 65.'

Jubb then reopened the question of a brittle fracture. Other experts argued that brittle fracture could only occur in low temperatures and not the 68°F of the Pacific. Jubb pointed out that there was evidence that the oil rig *Glomar Java Sea* had been proved to have been lost in 1983 through a brittle fracture at a high ambient sea temperature.

Shaun Kent, scrap metal merchant and possible owner of the wreck of the *Kowloon Bridge*, turned up with a large section of Frame 65 cut out by his divers. The inquiry was somewhat put out by this piece of metal, unloaded in the yard outside. 'That object or work of art troubles us a little,' said Gerald Darling. 'Is there any witness who can identify for certain that it is in fact Frame 65?'

The fracture mechanics expert, Dr Baker, duly obliged. That was on Day 40 when it was nearly all over.

Final submissions began and lasted for five days. As she sat in the public part of the Convocation Hall, Marion Baylis finally broke. When it was suggested on the forty-fifth day that the *Derbyshire* had not been in any heavy weather on her last voyage (before Cape Town), she shouted out that it was a lie. She knew: Curly had written to tell her, and the letter had come off with the last helicopter trip.

On the final day Belinda Bucknall, one of the Counsel for the relatives, apologised for Marion. It was the last humiliation for a dispirited group. Marion subsequently became very ill, an illness from which she has still not fully recovered.

The report was not published until 1989, a year later. The decision was this:

For the reasons stated in this report the Court finds that the *Derbyshire* was probably overwhelmed by the forces of nature in Typhoon Orchid, possibly after getting beam on to wind and sea, off Okinawa in darkness on the night 9th/10th September 1980 with the loss of forty-four lives. The evidence available does not support any firmer conclusion.

The Frame 65 failure, the shifting of the cargo or its 'liquefaction', the failure of hatch covers, all were dismissed. The main body of the report asserted that the ship had been built well.

As to the *Derbyshire*, Lloyd's had carried out 'calculations to determine the strength of the *Derbyshire*'s hull at Frame 65': it was found to conform with the computer-generated programme's permissible limits.

The rest of the quoted research all pointed away from failure due to fatigue, torsion, or brittle fracture. The brittle fractures on the other three ships (the *Kowloon Bridge* was not mentioned in this respect in the report) were 'noted' but the report simply asserted that:

> Brittle fractures, if initiated in the *Derbyshire*, would most probably have led to an arrested brittle crack in the deck with possible propagation down the longitudinal bulkheads into the sloping tankside [that is, endways, not across]. Complete fatigue failure and catastrophic fracture of the ship can be *ruled out* [our emphasis].

The report went on to details about possible hatch cover failure ('improbable'); flooding of forward compartments ('not . . . probable'); liquefaction ('not persuaded'); loss of engines ('cannot be completely discounted'); loss of steering ('cannot be discounted'); explosion ('extremely remote'); ingress of water due to pooping ('no evidence to substantiate such a hypothesis'); loss of directional stability (basically 'hmmm'); getting beam on to the seas ('cannot be precluded').

The *Kowloon Bridge*, the initiator of the inquiry does get one mention: 'The Court was told of an incident on a sister ship, the *Kowloon Bridge*, involving severe pooping . . . ' Not a word about her sinking, and why, not a hint of her role in the whole rolling caravan. But then if you decide to limit the scope of an inquiry on a vessel of which you have neither hide nor hair, and in which no witness is called from earlier crews, perhaps it is not so surprising that that old British favourite, the weather, gets the blame.

Looking at the transcripts, one is struck by several things. First, the complexity of the material put before the inquiry and the attendant problems of identifying what was being discussed (or even what document and what pages were being referred to). In this case people attending were expected to get to grips with the following: modern shipbuilding practices, welding technology, soil mechanics, fracture mechanics, hydrodynamics, mechanical and structural engineering, principles and practice – and the controversies over methods applied in these fields. Meteorology, ocean navigation, seamanship and the complexities of modern ship operations may have come as welcome breaks in all this.

12

Petition in Parliament

The formal inquiry report came as a severe blow to the families of the crew of the *Derbyshire*, now at least in touch with each other through the *Derbyshire* Families Association. And the realisation had grown among them that a shared unhappiness at least mitigated the anguish. Yet there came no relief, and by the end of 1989 all avenues seemed closed.

It was at this point that Tyne Tees Television took up the banner through their producer, Malcolm Wright, and the *Northern Eye* programme. The half-hour-long documentary, transmitted in June 1990, contained much of the material we have used in this book: there was an interview with Professor Bishop, for instance, about Frame 65.

By 1990 Dave Ramwell too had taken up the fight – incensed largely by the conclusions of the formal inquiry. Once more, after a considerable setback, folk like Peter Ridyard and Marion Baylis stirred themselves to action. This time a campaign to rouse public opinion seemed to be the only possible option.

In Liverpool, the home of eighteen of the dead crew, Eddie Loyden, one of the local Labour MPs, announced he would put down an Early Day motion in the House of Commons. It was signed eventually by seventy-seven MPs and it called for the reopening of the inquiry into the loss of the *Derbyshire*, noting the research of the Brunel University team. It added that the Wreck Commissioner, in the inquiry report, had said that different conclusions to those he had reached with his assessors could be applied if the kind of hull stresses the Brunel academics had argued did exist had been underestimated.

Fired by Loyden's actions Cathie Musa asked him if he could get her a copy of the 'draft' Department of Transport report of 1985, the one which said the most probable cause of the loss of the *Derbyshire* was through structural failure. Loyden asked the House of Commons Library for a copy only to find they did not have one, its circulation having been restricted to 'interested parties'. Cathie Musa then wrote to Loyden who was, by this simple means, able to put a question to the Secretary of State: 'To ask . . . if he will make available to the bereaved families of the crew of *Derbyshire* the draft report on the sinking of the vessel.'[1]

Patrick McLoughlin's reply said:

In January 1989, copies of the typescript Report of Court were distributed to the solicitors to the parties to the Formal Investigation into the loss of MV *Derbyshire*. Copies of the Supplemental Report and Order as to costs were distributed to the solicitors last month. At the Formal Investigation two firms of solicitors acted for dependants and those lost in the *Derbyshire* tragedy.[2]

It may be that there was genuine confusion over which 'draft' was being referred to. Later, when it was made quite clear it was the 1985 Department of Transport Report, it was still not formally available, as it is not to this day. As we saw in Chapter 11, this report was never discussed at the formal inquiry and the decision to exclude it was never challenged with the vigour that might have been expected. But it was perverse in the extreme for the Department to decline to make the draft available when copies are in circulation, in part via RMT, the Transport Workers' Union.

As long ago as May 1986 Ron Brown, MP had asked Nicholas Ridley, then Transport Secretary, if he would place a copy of this draft in the House of Commons Library. Ridley had replied: 'The document was an early draft . . . circulated only to interested parties for their comments. The draft was subsequently revised in the light of comments received and of further information which became available . . .'[3]

Peter Ridyard, Paul Lambert and others have each in turn been told by the Department of Transport that the place to raise the public reading of the draft was at the formal inquiry. There, the Wreck Commissioner, of course, ruled the report did not exist.

While the saga of the draft report was being played out on another stage, in the House of Commons the older battle continued. On October 26th, 1990 Eddie Loyden asked the Transport Secretary 'if he will now initiate an enquiry into the loss of MV *Derbyshire* and if he will make a statement'.[4]

McLoughlin replied that a formal investigation had taken place the year before but that 'new material' was being examined by the Marine Accident Investigation Branch (MAIB): 'Once they have concluded their investigations a report will be sent to the Secretary of State. After consideration of that report he will decide whether or not the formal investigation should be reopened.'[5]

Meanwhile in Liverpool the decision had been taken to gather signatures for a public petition to Parliament. Paul Lambert was coordinating the efforts for the North-West branch of the DFA. By November time was running out; the petition was due for presentation in mid-December. Eddie Loyden and Tony Santamera (for the RMT union) had been determined the petition should be strongly worded. It said:

> To the Honourable, the Commons of the United Kingdom of Great Britain and Northern Ireland in Parliament assembled. The humble petition of the *Derbyshire* Families Association sheweth: That in the light of new evidence on hull stressing and fatigue in large bulk carriers contained in a paper presented by Professor Geraint Price of Brunel University to the Royal Institute of Naval Architects on 18th October, 1990, and also the new evidence obtained by the Tyne Tees TV in underwater film of the wreckage of the *Kowloon Bridge*. Wherefore your petitioners pray that your honourable house urge the Secretary of State for Transport to establish a new public inquiry into the loss of MV *Derbyshire*. And your petitioners, as in duty bound, will ever pray, etc.

The campaigners believed they had irrefutable proof in the underwater film. It was this 'new evidence' that they hoped would prove decisive – even though it had been available during the time of the formal inquiry.

On Merseyside the press gave the petition the publicity its organisers craved. The story of the *Derbyshire* has never gone away in Liverpool and the surrounding towns: the ship had been registered there, she had carried the name *Liverpool Bridge* at the start of her life. Getting to the bottom of the story of her loss rang many bells in this north-western city.

The *Titanic* had been a Liverpool registered ship too, and the size comparisons – if not the loss of life – were a part of this identity. But, rightly or wrongly, the *Derbyshire* came to represent the way in which Liverpudlians saw the world: an example of the smug, uncaring south. The *Derbyshire* story had, up to the 1990s, lived up to that image.

A stall was set up in the city centre and a megaphone broadcast what was being asked for – signatures. Cathie Musa lost her voice that day and caught a bad cold but not even the loss of her voice, and the air coming off the Mersey like a cold flame, could stop her thrusting forms and ballpoint pen in front of passers-by.

Everyone became involved. Dave Ramwell's Second Engineer alone collected five hundred signatures. From the earlier despondent atmosphere, a feeling was growing that maybe, in the public's own simple responses, this time there would be a result.

In the House of Commons on December 6th Eddie Loyden stood up. Late in the parliamentary day it is permitted for short items to be raised, such as private notices or business questions, the introduction of new members, ministerial statements or, as Eddie Loyden hoped, a proposal to move the adjournment of the House 'on a specific and important matter that should have urgent consideration'.

The Speaker rules as to whether the application falls within the appropriate Standing Order. Even then, it must have the approval of those Members present or, if not, of at least forty MPs. Though any such motion is normally dealt with at the start of the next day's business, it may be taken the same evening, if its urgency is accepted.

Loyden began to tell the *Derbyshire* story. An ex-seaman, his experiences of that life enabled him to précis the complicated story in just one page of *Hansard*. He was backed by Roy Beggs, MP for Antrim East, one of whose constituents, Jimmy and Freda Kane's son, had been among the crew on the *Derbyshire*.

The government response came through the Under Secretary of State for Transport. 'It was a very important adjournment debate,' he began, only to continue: 'no material evidence came to light [during the formal inquiry] . . . the inquiry was independent and wide-ranging . . . concluded that the *Derbyshire* was properly designed, properly built and that materials of approved standard were used.' The House adjourned at eleven minutes to eleven o'clock.

Outside the battle to get as many signatures as possible for the petition continued. To present that petition a small posse from Liverpool came to London, Dave Ramwell among them. This is his account written at the time:

It wasn't as though I didn't want to attend the House of Commons for the presentation, it was just that I thought the day belonged to the relatives of those who had been lost in the ship. My first indications of any reluctance were jumped on by Cathie Musa who threatened to drag me into the van – I was delighted that she and the others felt my place was with them.

Originally, we were told, the presentation was to be in the afternoon of December 14th, a Friday. But then the Rev Ken Peters of the Mersey Mission to Seamen phoned: 'It is now at nine o'clock in the morning. We will have to leave Lime Street at 4 a.m. Are you still wanting to go?'

I asked him to check again with the relatives and when he phoned back he just said, 'We're all mad.' I could see his smile as clearly as if he were standing next to me. I parked my car at a relatively safe place in Liverpool. It had its own built-in protection, anyway – who would want to steal an old car?

It was cold outside Lime Street station in mid-December. A car pulled up beside me. I recognised Ros Blease. Her son had brought her. He and his brother had lost their father when Tom was just thirty, over ten years ago now.

I wished the van would arrive; it wasn't just the cold. A tall, moustached, bespectacled man was marching up and down the taxi rank, military fashion, and giving his orders. The shabbiness of his dress parodied the smartness of his parade and orders, as he delivered self-commands: about turn, left, right. The slouched taxi-drivers watching him suggested they had seen it all before. But he was swearing and sailors are embarrassed – believe it or not – if a man swears in front of a woman.

I became nervous when he did an 'about turn' and marched up to Ros. But all he asked for was a cigarette. When he saw my growing irritation he backed away, ordered a quick about turn and a quick march, into the night. His departure was marked by the arrival of two more bound for London with us, Eric McAlenan and Ted Leatherbarrow, between them responsible for thousands of the signatures we had collected.

Soon after them the Mission mini-bus arrived. Reverends Ken Peters and Peter McGrath were the two drivers. Already aboard were Cathie, Helen Burke, Margaret Noblett and a new face to me, Norma Sutton.

To sit in a van where scousers make up the better part of the passenger list is – if you are not yourself a scouser – to be amused for the whole journey. Most Liverpudlians have the talent for injecting humour into the most impossible situations. The journey south, long though it was, entailed not one dull minute. That included the stop at a service station for a cup of tea and a snowball fight!

I had suggested to Ken that he contacted the Dreadnought Unit at St Thomas' Hospital across the Thames, as a place we might be able to leave the van; they agreed we could. So it was only a short walk for our little party to the House of Commons once we had arrived.

We warmed ourselves in a nearby café, then made our way through the strict security checks to meet Eddie Loyden. He led us to the central lobby where, a little later, John Prescott, shadow Transport Minister, came to meet us. From there we went to the Visitors' Gallery. Looking down, we all remarked how small the chamber looked – no doubt as thousands have before. I noticed the distance between the two front benches – the distance between two drawn swords, I believe.

Eddie presented the petition – close on 47,000 signatures. It was all very ritualistic and quaint, but necessary, I suppose, to keep anarchy at bay. Linda Chalker began to speak and we left. According to the plan we met Eddie and John Prescott and walked across to Downing Street where the relatives of *Derbyshire's* lost men, escorted by the two MPs, presented the petition to No. 10. ITN recorded it for that evening's local news.

We went back to the van on the other side of the river, our earlier buoyancy fading. The journey back was uneventful to begin with but as we got closer to home darkness and then fog descended. Ken was driving when the van's demisters gave up. I was nervously aware he had been up for something like thirty hours. In the back no one spoke; tiredness and cold bodies went together with, by now, numbed minds. It had been a very long day.

To date this was the 'last throw' by the DFA and its friends. No change of government thinking occurred. The Department of Transport continued to examine the evidence but effectively kept any thought of a reopening of the formal inquiry at more than arm's length. The reading of the Brunel team research results to RINA in 1990 did not lead to more than a short-term flurry of interest.

Some among the DFA were by now sick and tired of the whole business. Nearly eleven years had passed by then and still there was no end in sight. Yet there was a development – one which was by late 1991 to become a sensational story. That was the casualty list for large bulk carriers in the 1980s. Over 200 had been lost, the majority of them in equally mysterious circumstances to that of the *Derbyshire*.

In mid-1991 people in the international shipping industry were beginning to worry in public about what might be going on. By late 1991 Lloyd's Register was changing its own methods of survey for bulkers.

13

Losses in Bulk

While the saga of the *Derbyshire* has been running, another much bigger story was emerging through the 1980s. By the autumn of 1991 this other story had become sufficiently large for *Lloyd's List*, the shipping paper, to run a special investigation headlined with dramatic simplicity, 'Vanishing bulkers'.

The facts are startling. Since 1975 more than 280 bulk carriers had been lost to one cause or another; thirty had been listed as missing, lost or damaged in the period January 1990 to September 1991. The *Lloyd's List* editorial of September 17th, 1991, said this:

> Mariners, shipbuilders, metallurgists, naval architects, classification societies and insurers are all agreed that there are serious problems with bulk carriers, *particularly older vessels lifting heavy ores* [our emphasis]. Nearly 300 seafarers have lost their lives in the past 20 months in accidents which have, for the most part, been impossible to attribute to heavy weather or human error.[1]

In 1990, again more than half the number lost (57 per cent) was accounted for by bulk and combination carriers; yet of 78,336 ships it was, at 5156 ships, only 7 per cent of the total (although 31 per cent by tonnage). At a Lloyd's symposium held in May 1991, Lloyd's own officials admitted that thirty-four bulk carrier casualties since the beginning of 1990 were due to *structural weakness* (our emphasis). In the period 1975 to 1990 world total losses were 3302 ships (of 21,438,824 gross tons). Of these, bulk and combination carriers accounted for 279 ships (of 5,866,841 gross tons), or 27 per cent of the total, an average over the period of seventeen ships a year. One case, which typified what had been happening, was that of the 170,000 tonne *Mineral Diamond*, British managed and Belgian owned. It was certainly true that most of the ships lost were older; there was a continuing reluctance to see the *Derbyshire*, when she was mentioned, as other than 'atypical'. But the *Mineral Diamond*, which, like the *Derbyshire*, just disappeared (in April 1991), was well-maintained and nearly new.

Built in 1982, she was last heard of on April 17th, 1200 miles west of Australia, and steaming towards a gale at half speed, making 6.5 knots in very rough seas. She was carrying 136,000 tonnes of iron ore and twenty-six Indian officers and crew. In the same month as she vanished, three other bulkers went down.

At the subsequent inquiry instituted by the Hong Kong Director of Marine, it was suggested the ship might have been encountering wave heights of 60 feet. The investigation conclusion reads:

Due to the failure to find the wreckage or survivors, the precise cause of her loss remains uncertain. In the absence of any other *plausible* [our emphasis] explanation, it seems most likely that a major structural failure of her hull, which resulted in her breaking in two, is the cause of her sinking.[2]

Relatives of the crew of the *Derbyshire* were quick to point out that if you swapped the names of the ships, you had the story of the *Derbyshire* uncannily reproduced, just under eleven years on.

Three other casualties in 1990 were 'typical' to the authorities collecting data. In March an elderly Capesize, *Alexandre-P*, built in 1967, oil/ore carrier with a crew of twenty-four, left Dampier in Australia, where she had loaded iron ore. She was never seen again, the only trace being two burnt corpses in a wrecked lifecraft and some small wreckage. It is thought she sank within forty-eight hours of leaving port, in fine weather.

A few months later the 170,000 dwt oil/ore carrier *Algarrobo* left the Chilean iron ore port of Huasco bound for Japan. She was never seen again; in this case no trace was found. The weather was fine in the Pacific. Finally in this sorry saga the 155,000 dwt *Pasithea* vanished without trace off Kagoshima.

Not long after, another bulker, the *Gallant Dragon*, having been brought back to the Brazilian port of Tubarao already sinking with a full cargo of iron ore, was scuttled when she was deemed too badly damaged to save. She took a matter of seconds to sink.

The events of 1991 seemed destined to revive the story of the *Derbyshire*. It was the sinking of the *Mineral Diamond* which began the international panic over bulk carriers, and panic is the correct word to use.

The irony will not be lost on the reader. We believe literally hundreds of lives could have been saved, millions of tons of cargo not lost, hundreds of millions in insurance not paid out, if the lessons of the *Derbyshire* and many other bulk carriers had been learned earlier. Those lessons were not just about the Bridge class of ships. The bigger, broader picture is that bulk carriers, in the nature of what they are and what they do, are highly vulnerable to certain kinds of problem. One of these is slamming in heavy seas, linked to the stresses outlined by the Bishop, Price and partners research: another is brittle fracture under certain conditions. But there are more – one authority has identified as many as twenty-one problems.

The effect of the rising graph of bulk carrier casualties on seafaring was electric. As the summer of 1991 wore on, more and more shipmasters came forward to tell their stories of bulk carrier operations. Like the lid being lifted on Pandora's box, these often terrifying accounts of life in bad weather on a large bulker provoked a gale of comment and counter-comment. Conferences were hastily arranged, classification societies rushed to amend their rules, to do more research.

Behind this was a greater worry. If large bulkers – especially older ones, of which there are an increasing proportion in the world fleet – are vulnerable, how will this affect a world economy afflicted by recession? By how much, and how fast, will prices of raw materials rise? If even part of the underlying story as to why these ships are sinking is right, we may be facing the biggest crisis in world shipping since the Second World War.

Because the issue has so many ramifications it is important to understand as much of the debate as possible. Like the discussion of stresses in large ships, this is not a straightforward issue. There are disagreements a-plenty. What was interesting about the developments in 1991, however, was the unanimity of opinion that *something* was seriously wrong, and that structural questions had to be forcefully addressed, as did questions of corrosion (by cargoes), over-rapid loading and discharge of cargoes, and, crucially, the way ships were passed after survey.

At the same time, the behaviour of large ships is not always what a layman might expect. Writing in the *Seaways* journal of the Nautical Institute in May 1991, Captain Eric Beetham, former shipmaster and vice president of the Institute, said:

When we fly on an aircraft, I'm sure we have all seen the wings lift as they take the weight of the body on taking off and we have seen the wings flap about quite cheerfully in turbulence. What few of us have seen, or even know of, is the regular replacement of the section of shell plating extending under an aircraft fuselage in way of the wings. In a similar way all of us at sea have seen the bending of a ship in heavy weather or the heavy – sometimes violent – movement that can result from wave-induced vibration acting on the hull as a girder. This can take the bridge, at the top of the superstructure, forward and back by a few feet and the fo'c'sle up and down many feet. Unlike the aircraft, no shell plating is replaced.

Beetham went on to ask why all these bulk carriers might have sunk. He was careful not to be provocative but, in discussing the loading of oil/ore carriers (a simpler version of an OBO), he said:

> To avoid shut out of cargo [through the ship sagging under its loading] we whacked the ore into the aftermost hold [number nine on the Bridge class] to prevent the sag and the result was that stresses were above 95 per cent of the allowable figure [see Diagram 1, p. 139]. The point of maximum stress was immediately in front of the bridge – any fracture there that let the ship break in two would have resulted in an immediate sinking of the stern section.

He said there were two real differences between the ore carrier and the bulk carrier. First, the ore carrier is classed to load alternate holds while not all bulk carriers are; second, ore carriers usually have a better deadweight/draught relationship (that is, when loaded they are higher out of the water). He pointed out that the losses had two features: one, that those ships lost were usually old; second, that they were carrying heavy cargoes.

This led to a simple question: were the weight distribution and associated stresses, allowed for when the ship was young, still valid when she was older? Speed of loading (of which we have more to say below) was also critical:

> . . . the change in attitude (of the ship) during the loading is very considerable. The final state does not really come until after the ship has sailed and the structure settled – we have all seen this when loading in North Africa and sailing with a hog, only to arrive in Italy two or three days later and find the loadline is down as the result of the hog having changed to a sag.

More damningly, Beetham pointed out that waving about ultrasonic test reports to argue that a particular ship was in good condition was irrelevant. It all depended on where in the ship the tests were taking place. Using the aircraft analogy he said that testing the wing roots told you nothing about the wing shell plating: 'Is it fair wear and tear when, a month after special survey, a section of shell plating falls off or when the decks are showing darkly-rusted edges to large fractures? This happens increasingly often . . .'

Perhaps Beetham's most telling comments were about driving ships too hard. He thought that as a ship grew older the standard of hull survey had to be much more thorough. The only way to do that was to get in among the ship's structure and look – frequently. A landlubber may be astonished that this is not done. It is as if, passing a car chassis fit for an MoT, a car mechanic merely glanced over the bodywork.

Beetham believed, despite his comments about ageing bulkers, that the cause of the *Derbyshire* loss 'would appear to have been a structural failure in way of the aft coffer dam. The arguments raised by Bishop and Price suit the circumstances and may have some substance in this particular case.'[3]

More generally, loss of shell plating (the sides of ships falling off), failure of structure due to wastage, excessive local loading, inadequate survey and maintenance, driving too hard in bad weather and frequent use of ballast in uncoated spaces all added to probable causes. Many of the ships had been old (81 per cent of recent casualties were either due for, or past, their third special survey). This led inexorably to fatigue fractures.

In June 1991 the Southampton Master Mariners' Club held its annual meeting. The discussion was: 'Bulk carriers: ships safe to sail in?' Among those attending were Peter Ridyard and Captain Peter Marriott, the Marine Accident Investigation Branch chief inspector.

The meeting heard that it had been the poor economic conditions of the 1980s which squeezed shipowners into not maintaining ships so well. Owners had delayed, curtailed or even cancelled essential work. The results, one speaker felt, were now manifest in the casualty statistics. The ships most at risk were those in the twelve- to fifteen-year-old range.

Peter Ridyard believed the prime cause of the unexplained total losses (of which there were many) were failures of design, of construction and of structure caused by corrosion and heavy weather stresses. He thought the fact that there were no distress signals in many cases of total loss suggested sudden and massive structural failure.

He also added that with the demise of the British shipbuilding industry fewer and fewer competent surveyors were available. Many now lacked practical experience and many of the classification societies were forced to employ graduates lacking basic shipbuilding knowledge. To be of any use, ship survey standards had to be uniform and reliable. As classification societies were competing for the same tonnage, he believed standards had suffered. He also felt much more had to be done to teach ship's crews to detect and recognise early signs of structural deterioration.

Another speaker to the meeting, Brian Corlett, told the audience that of eighteen bulk/ore, bulk/oil or OBOs lost between January 1990 and April

1991, fourteen were carrying iron ore. He pointed out that this cargo meant high bending moments and shear forces which varied along the ship's length. Loading rates at some terminals had increased dramatically (see Diagram 1, p. 139) and, along with a question mark over a hull's ability to withstand rapidly changing loads in a ship's holds, there was the issue of damage by the cargo (or the grabs) on the hold structure.

The meeting – particularly the shipmasters who spoke – was highly critical of current standards and practices. One speaker wondered whether unscrupulous owners were not deliberately scuttling ships, attributing the loss to structural failure and then collecting the insurance money. Another master mariner commented that he had seen many reports from masters to owners, 'even "blue chip" owners', utterly disregarded even on a second or third time of reporting. Two others said they had seen ships passed by surveyors despite extensive and serious corrosion. One master knew of a ship which had been switched from one classification society to another with the express purpose of evading the class requirements. Another said he had experience of a class surveyor renewing a safety equipment certificate after a 'perfunctory' thirty-minute survey.

The debate in Southampton was being mirrored in many other places. Ship's masters (let alone their officers and crew) tend to be conservative when it comes to speaking out. Conditions at sea have always been harsh and seafarers pride themselves on coping even in bad circumstances. All have been worried by the shipping slump and are anxious to keep their jobs. It is all the more surprising, then, to find the upsurge of letter-writing and public statement-making by these same men. The relief at being able to share in these worries is palpable.

But it was a surveyor, Mr McDowell, writing in *Seaways* in August 1991, who had some of the most startling information. He mentioned several cases of bulk carriers:

An ore carrier, built about 1974 . . . When reaching the final stages of discharge, cargo was found to be running through the bulkhead from No. 6 to No. 7 and later from No. 2 to No. 3 [holds]. Closer inspection revealed that the lower third of both transverse bulkheads was totally corroded; in fact it was possible to stand on the tank-top and see the engine room bulkhead from No. 1 hold. In addition, not one ballast tank could be filled to capacity due to splits and holes at varying heights.

An ore carrier built in 1971 . . . The slightest touch of the grabs on the hold sides resulted in holing of the plating, flooding of the cargo spaces with ballast water and consequent problems of discharging mud-like ore. The repair crew was continuously employed welding patches.

An OBO built in 1971 . . . an inspection revealed that in No. 3 hold, of 20 frames on the starboard side, all 20 were totally separated from the shell plating for their whole height and were only prevented from flapping about by the 25mm bolts which had been used to secure the lower extremities to knees at the top of the hopper slope. This hold had been loaded with 23,000 mt of ore and it was the intention of the chief officer to ballast this hold to 40 per cent . . . The upper wing tanks were not used for ballast, one can imagine why!

Captain Lanham, writing in the same journal in September 1991, said that he had

always been amazed where we were allowed to use partially filled holds for ballast in seagoing conditions. As a young apprentice, intrigued by the crash and shudder of the ship as the water in the ballast hold moved from side to side, we opened the deck access trap hatch to have a look. We were amazed to see the five-metre comber rolling from side to side and it was only when a larger roll threw spray up around us that we quickly got out and dogged down the lid.

He went on to point out the kind of damage this could result in:

On one voyage a corrugated bulkhead of the ballast hold pulled away from the ship's side plating, flooding the adjacent hold. A few years further on, one of the transverse side frames in the ballast hold partially tore off the side shell and coiled itself up like a spring. It was only then when a cherry picker hoist was placed in the hold and close examination of the side frames could be carried out that the extent of the problem was evident. All frames in the ballast holds were wafer thin. All had to be replaced. The corrosion was accelerated by the constant stressing of the frames caused by the ballast water movement. The ship at this time was *six years old* [our emphasis].

Captain Lanham suggested a major issue was the sheer size of these ships. The work involved in proper checking of all tanks or holds, apart from the difficulty of access without scaffolding, was enormous. Yet, he pointed out:

We have all attended class surveys and you are standing in the bottom of the hold looking up. The steelwork is covered in dust with plenty of evidence of normal wear and tear. But unless framing is hanging off or badly bent it looks OK. The depth of hold and distance away from the steelwork makes it impossible to gauge the severity of corrosion.[4]

What Captain Lanham is describing is a little like standing in a cathedral nave and looking up and assessing the condition of the roof beams.

While the debate raged among seafarers, both classification societies and a host of experts rushed to make some kind of judgment. Many wrote in *Seaways* because the Nautical Institute, its parent body, is the *primus inter pares* arbiter of international seafaring safety. Mr Brooking, a naval architect, writing in August, believed that bulk carriers spent a significant amount of time sailing at the extremes of the operational draught range. Unlike tankers, however, 'the side structure . . . form torsion boxes to compensate for the loss of torsional rigidity caused by the presence of hatch openings. The compensation can result in high reserves of strength for vertical bending . . . [which] . . . explains why bulk carriers are seen to flex less than tankers.' Put another way, their extra stiffness is dangerous because of the stresses it induces. He felt that 'fatigue cracking and brittle fracture . . . very often linked together . . . may be the cause of many losses'.[5]

What of Lloyd's Register? Also writing in the same issue of *Seaways* was Mr Ferguson of Lloyd's Register's technical planning and development department. By the summer of 1991 Lloyd's Register was clearly more than worried by what had been happening. Ferguson said that:

It has become increasingly apparent that dry bulk carriers are the heavy workhorses of the world fleet and, because of their cargoes, could inadvertently experience loadings not normally catered for in their design . . . Recent events, however, in the form of major damage to a number of bulk carriers, some of which were constructed in the last decade, led Lloyd's Chief Ship Surveyor to giving priority to a study with a view to determining the probable causes.[6]

It was in November 1990 that Lloyd's Register started a special bulk carrier study. At the same time they issued special instructions to surveyors to look closely at holds and, in particular, main frames and brackets. This was followed almost immediately by a press release advising of corrosion and cracking problems.

By January 1991 they were giving additional 'guidance' to surveyors of bulkers and writing to bulk carrier owners and operators, 'portraying concern'. A month later they were writing to owners, 'drawing attention to untypically high rate(s) of casualties'. In April they asked for a close-up inspection on a sample of bulk carriers as part of the study and found that many owners believed that cracking in the structure of bulk carriers was inevitable, possibly as a result of poor design and, more probably, because of the way the ships are run.

Lloyd's Register has 17,000 sets of data for ships built since 1960 to class rules, or which have been classed later at Lloyd's. Many of those data relate to bulkers and their designs, including the Bridge class.

'It became evident that corrosion and cracking of the main frames and their brackets is a significant occurrence,' one of their number wrote in *100A1*, the Lloyd's Register journal, in 1991. Given that this is the society which surveys ships we find it amazing that the corrosion and cracking damage now highlighted on every page, the subject of every casual discussion by classification society surveyors, was a surprise to them.

In the late autumn Patrick McLoughlin, then Shipping Minister, addressed the International Maritime Organisation. Among other things he condemned the failure of classification societies to carry out proper surveys. One of them, he said, (not Lloyd's) had offered to classify a ship by fax, without bothering to inspect it at all. McLoughlin said it could no longer be accepted that every classification society gave priority to safety.

Lloyd's List in a November 1991 leader, indeed praised the Register for recognising the crisis and then gathering information about it, thus enabling action to be taken. For this they deserve credit. But our fundamental criticism, developed more in Chapter 14, is over the time it has taken for any recognition that there might be a fundamental problem (bulkers have been sinking for years, on an annually increasing trend) and the reluctance still to examine *all* the evidence in public.

Before we close this chapter, it is worth looking at what the pressures of bulk ship operation can be, in order that we may assess the depth of the problem. For years casualties were passed off as maverick, untypical, or just mysteries (like the *Derbyshire*). The *Lloyd's List* special investigation into what they described as 'vanishing' bulkers said: 'Commercial pressures dictating the growth of ship size for the carriage of low-value commodities such as ore, have also dictated that cargoes be handled at ever-increasing speeds'. The paper pointed out that many operators, acting under these basic pressures, were 'less than circumspect, not only about the speed at which they allow their vessels to be loaded to their full deadweight, but also as regards the pattern of loading'.[7]

The decision on the speed of loading ultimately rests with the ship master, who is under enormous pressure to load as fast as possible (to avoid excess port charges).

This may well mean that down the years the hull structure can be fatally affected. When the Hamersley Iron shiploaders at Dampier in Australia can load ore at a rate of 9000 and 7500 tonnes an *hour* and in Tubarao, Brazil similar machines can load at 16,000 tonnes an hour, the temptation must be to load at maximum speed.

Good ship operators limited the loads their ships embarked, and the rate at which they loaded. Some made allowance for sea-stresses likely to be encountered, rather than those calculated for calm water in harbour. With ore cargoes there has always been another problem. That is, because the cargo is so dense it does not fill the holds. This means the sideplating is not supported (think of a shopping bag part-filled with potatoes) and it also means that the 'stiffness' of the ship will rise, leading, as we have seen, to much worse bending and shearing forces at sea.

Behind the worries over loading of bulk cargoes has lain the knowledge that they are generally the overworked, under-maintained Cinderellas of the sea. In fact insurance underwriters have long understood this from the figures they see annually, and have identified the heart of the issue to lay with neglect, poor management and operation. Elderly vessels which sink have relatively modest value and pose low liability risk, however, so they can still get insurance.

Until recently there has not been much commercial concern. A fifteen-year-old bulker of 80,000 tons deadweight might carry a hull value below $10 million and a cargo of $3.5 million. A total loss of a ship like this would be considered – financially – routine (compared with a tanker, say).

Tanker losses have another dimension: public fury over pollution. A quarter of a million tons of ore does not make a headline in environmental terms. But by the end of 1991 there were growing worries among underwriters that what they might be facing in the 1990s was an ageing fleet (including more and more tankers) which was simply falling apart.

One suggestion for a 'quick fix' for the industry to escape the inevitable was the compulsory fitting of strain gauges and accelerometers on older bulkers, which would give those on the bridge an indication when stress levels were rising to dangerous levels. It was discovered, however, that this equipment might not be able to detect the worst kinds of stresses and that it might even give a false sense of security.

Another suggestion was that older bulkers should be required to have internal sand-blasting and renewal of coatings, but although this would pick up corrosion problems it would be very costly to implement. Cost was still overriding all other concerns among owners.

One problem still bedevilled many of the discussions: the causes of the losses. It was clear, for example, that there was no single cause: wastage, stress, weather, handling, or cargo damage had all been put forward.

Bureau Veritas, a classification society, pondered whether 'bulk carriers have a limited life beyond which they became unsafe', only to say it was a premature conclusion to reach.

Quite likely a whole variety of factors are involved, although there may well be common threads. Bulk carriers were a logical outcome of earlier ship types, the single deckers which were built with double bottoms, hopper tanks, single transversely-framed side shells, topside tanks and deck hatchways. These ships began at about 20,000 tons deadweight in the 1960s; they have been stretched – without major changes in configuration – to vessels of 170,000 tons deadweight.

The problems overall have been isolated – even though their significance is argued about. The large hatch spaces reduce torsional resistance and attract stress – particularly at the corners. Hatch coamings are prone to cracking, and cracking has also been identified at the intersection of the inner bottom plating and the hopper plating (see Diagram 2, p. 140).

There is both general and local corrosion of main frames and brackets, cracking at main frame bracket toes, and cracking at fore and aft extremities of topside tanks. We have already discussed cargo handling damage – the grabs may weigh up to 35 tons apiece. The effect of one of these hitting a ship's side may well be imagined, loaded or not. Sometimes bulldozers are used to help clear the holds, and again one can envisage the potential for damage to a ship's structure.

If coal has been carried the resulting dust concentrations may require pneumatic hammers to clean the surfaces, with probable damage to the ship. Eric Beetham has already been quoted on the way these ships are bent up and down during loading sequences. Concern over the design has been expressed by, among others, Harland and Wolff chairman, John Parker, who has said that he does not believe modern bulk carriers have sufficient built-in redundancy of structure to cope with wear and tear.

Harland and Wolff are building a new class of large bulk carriers in 1992. They have made plain that they will be building them to much higher standards. By November 1991, after a year in which international shipping had been racked with the debate over bulk carriers, Lloyd's Register also announced tougher rules to keep bulk carriers in class.

The society's technical committee approved changes to, for example, side structure to cover minimum strength and thickness for frames and brackets; recommendations for detailed design and welding of brackets, with an increased weld factor; requirements for higher tensile steel frames and brackets; additional requirements for supporting structures in hopper and topside tanks; higher tensile steel frames and brackets will require fabricated T sections with integral brackets.

They are also to insist on new requirements for watertight bulkheads: average strengths to be increased by 20 to 30 per cent (a quarter to a third), and weld factors to be increased at bulkhead boundaries so that they are of equal strength to bulkhead plating. Lloyd's asked for these changes to be made by April 1992.

Lloyd's reported that their study of bulk carrier losses had established that mechanical damage to the side shell structure in holds during cargo working made the ships vulnerable to shell failure in heavy weather, especially when corrosion was present. We believe they have, therefore, accepted evidence on structural failure. They also believed their regraded rules might put them 'out on a limb'[8] with respect to other classification societies.

The last word here ought to go to *Lloyd's List* in a leader they wrote in October 1991:

This sort of crisis needs some powerful action, rather than pious hopes and a general distribution of blame that emerges from the maritime industry itself . . . in this fragmented business of maritime transport where cargo loaders know nothing of ship structural strength, and charterers believe that ships run on rails, a meeting where some of the home truths of bulk carrier construction, operation and maintenance can be aired must be a worthwhile occasion.

But whether the conclusions would satisfy those who grieve for relatives lost at sea in these giant and seemingly invulnerable ships seems very doubtful. These people want action, they want governments to act in what they perceive as a major scandal which seems to be doing nothing to stop the loss of lives. They want to stop other bulkship seamen joining their dead relatives on the ocean floor. It is all very well lecturing shipbuilders about scantlings, and hoping that stevedores do not bend the ships like bananas. It is all very well classification societies adjusting their rules and recommending owners to have a look at the internals of their older bulk ships. But there is a real lack of commitment in this sort of action that seems to depend on good will as much as anything else.

Teeth are urgently needed to compel owners to get older ships to shipyards where they can be surveyed properly by experts using adequate access equipment.[9]

To the kind of teeth that are needed in international shipping to make bulk carriers safe – all bulk carriers, whatever their age or cargo – we now finally turn.

14

Time for Change

Things have started to move at last. We are witnessing the start of a worldwide trend – the *recognition* of the problem that bulk carriers, under a whole range of conditions, can be unsafe to operate. The pity is that it has taken so long.

Douglas Foy, retired mariner and former secretary of the Marine Institute, compiled a list of seventy bulk carriers thought lost to heavy weather and structural failure in the mid-1980s. Dave Ramwell has compiled another from Hook's *Modern Shipping Disasters, 1963–87*; others had warned that these workhorses of the sea have singular problems not faced by other types of vessels.

Today – even after the events of 1991 – the marine industry is reluctant to take certain uncomfortable truths on board. This is particularly true of the classification societies. The reason why is easy to find. They are caught on the horns of a dilemma and, under the present system, there can be no escape. On the one hand they set rules of conduct, and on the other, they are paid to pass as fit the operators of those rules – paid by those same operators. There's the rub.

Foy, writing in *Fairplay International*, said:

There is no conspiracy of silence. There is, however, a practice of silence as follows.

The ship's classification society will remain silent regarding the condition of the ship at its last survey. Any other classification society which refused to class the ship will remain silent as to the reasons it refused class.

The Salvage Association, which investigates a ship's loss, will report only to the underwriters and will remain silent if approached by other, interested, parties.

The ship's owners will remain silent on any defects on the ship, the manning or the management, which may have contributed to the disaster.

Flag state investigators conducting a preliminary inquiry into a loss will normally remain silent on their findings.

Finally, silence is practised regarding the beneficial owner of a ship. The owner's name, as published, may be a 'brass plate' name.

The silence of organisations and governments helps to keep potential death ships in service and contributes to the loss of between 100 and 150 bulk carrier seafarers every year.[1]

The cynical might remark at this point that unconcern in the west over the fate of these seafarers might be related to their being almost exclusively Third World citizens. This should not be so. Neither should the axiom which appears to dominate international shipping that if profit is at loggerheads with safety, the former will win.

Bad practices at sea have always been an endemic likelihood. Ships leave port; they all disappear in a sense and what goes on during a voyage is very much out of sight to those who regulate on the land. Ship law has often been horribly harsh; justice rough. Seafarers down the centuries have realised that their common foe was not so much the sea as the landsiders who would have them risk all for nought.

Regulation of shipping tends to come late and it has always come as a reluctant addition to practices which, time and again, shipowners have insisted are the only way to keep going. The Plimsoll Line on ships – their loading marks – came after Victorian sailors lost their lives in coffin ships. Even that system of regulation can be literally bent as we have seen.

Lifeboats sufficient to take an entire ship's company came only after the *Titanic* sank, and, one is forced to wonder, would that have come about if so many prominent passengers had not been aboard. Even so, efforts were made to blame any but the White Star Line's chairman, Lord Ismay, who recklessly encouraged his captain to speed through an icefield.

Shipping firms have not been all bad but, overall, they do not come across as good employers. In the First World War, when a ship was torpedoed all ship's company pay was stopped *from the moment the ship was deemed to have sunk* – not the actions of sympathetic management. You cannot legislate compassion but, perhaps, if the other rules are changed it might force those who live on land to take more account of the risks still taken willingly by those who go to sea.

We are not arguing, for one moment, that shipping can be made a completely safe business. The oceans of the world continue to exercise their awesome power. Shipping is a risky business, part of the attraction. It goes further than that. What captain is going to complain about 'superficial' deck cracks if the complaint is going to cost him his job? With pressures mounting to load faster and sail sooner, when bigger ships are earning record rates, what shoreside manager dares suggest a corroded bulker be taken out of service for extensive and expensive repairs? What owner is going to upset the charterer by reducing the amount of cargo carried?

Yet we are all to blame. Charterers will argue: what consumer wishes to pay maybe twice as much for goods in the shops? Crudely then, a couple of hundred dead sailors and the compensation (not that there is much) paid to their grieving relatives is a small price to pay for a world dedicated to obtaining the cheapest of raw materials, carried in vast ships largely for our benefit.

What is needed is a two-pronged attack on current practices. The obstacle to implementation is that the shipping industry is the most internationalised of all, the embryo for the world common market. It has been like that for at least a hundred years when it was all run by the British. Many of the best practices came out of that policing role; so did some of the worst.

We still have a tendency in Britain to blame all the bad practices on the rest of the world. Lloyd's Register believes it is the best of the classification societies and the best rule maker. No doubt British shipbuilding firms will continue to argue that they are the best, as will shipping companies too. The number of British ships has declined to a very low level, whatever beneficial ownership still remains. We are no longer truly a maritime nation, having turned our back on deep-sea trades for Europe, nearly two decades ago. That has been part of the problem. Just as we no longer build the world's great ships – and are unlikely ever to do so again – so we have to adjust our sights downwards.

The key change that is needed is the removal of the shipping industry's over-reliance on self-regulation. Interviewed in 1991 on the BBC's World Service *Seven Seas* programme, Paul Slater, chairman of First International Capital (a shipping finance house) said:

> The shipping industry's inspection requirements are not dictated nor enforced by law; they tend to be generated and dominated by the requirements of the shipping insurance industry that established, many years ago, organisations called classification societies who certify both the design and construction and operation of ships – and they physically inspect them. The problem we have is that these classification societies are independent and competitive with each other for their services and are therefore profit oriented.

He continued:

> It is essential that we have government intervention in the issuing of licences and certificates at all levels of shipping, from licensing a shipping company to certifying the quality of the crew, to regularly inspecting and certifying the ships, and such an authority would take the form of the Civil Aviation Authority or Federal Aviation Authority that do such a good job in the aircraft business.[2]

Nevertheless we are still 'big' in shipping finance and it is here that real influence from Lloyd's Register, from the underwriters and ship managers, from the Department of Transport and the Department of Trade could be of great influence. The UN body for shipping, the International Maritime Organisation, is based in London; the Nautical Institute is there too, and of considerable importance.

If the European Community, Japan and the United States alone moved in this direction we believe it would provide the impetus for others to follow. It would transform the current situation in shipping and would substantially increase safety at sea, and reduce casualties. We think the truth, the unhappy truth, is that the classification society system no longer works in today's fiercely competitive environment. It should be ended.

There are something approaching 10,000 bulk carriers operating today, worldwide. Of these about a third, 3500, are over fifteen years old. As we have seen, one of the more likely causes of failure is corrosion through the use of high tensile steel which, being stronger than mild steel, can be used in smaller scantlings. A report by the US Coastguard of 1990 said: 'Cause of structural failures. Poorly designed details, poor weld workmanship, and fatigue appear to be the major causes of structural degradation.'[3] What is startling is that this report was not about bulk carriers but about *tankers*.

If oil tankers began to fail at the rate bulk carriers do, you may be sure that things would change at very high speed. The implications for the world economy would be horrendous – as would the pollution. It would be the latter which would trigger the first public outcry, followed by howls of protest as petrol prices rocketed. Bulk cargoes, being low grade, low value, have not had any impact on the pollution front, nor yet on the price front.

In the end nothing will change dramatically until these bulk carriers are built better, and to higher standards. Harland and Wolff have promised this is what they will be doing with their new ships. Up to now, with the shipping slump of the 1980s, builders worldwide have been under pressure to reduce their costs by building bulkers to minimum weight. At the same time the rapid increase in size of bulk carriers through the 1960s and 1970s seems to have resulted in ships just being stretched and stretched.

The use of high tensile steel is still a matter for fierce debate, with plenty of people in the industry prepared to defend its use. Japanese shipbuilders have said of late that their research suggests it could not be blamed for shell plate cracking; some university research has implied that choices of steel are far from simple. What we do know is that high tensile steel, while being lighter, is less able to cope with wastage from corrosion.

There has been concern as to whether modern bulkers are designed to ensure sufficient 'redundancy' of structure in the case of damage, as well as the question of fatigue strength in critical areas (which, as we have seen, are themselves a matter for dispute). In a paper presented to the international general committee of Bureau Veritas it was said that modern fatigue analysis was now able to calculate fatigue strengths of structure much more precisely. The paper suggested 'stricter constructional standards to high tensile steel should be required.'[4] It went on to say that proper long-life, anti-corrosion systems had to be built in to ships, especially in vulnerable areas like ballast spaces. The efficiency of such systems would have to be regularly checked.

Part of this checking involves crawling around the ship's insides. The problem of physical access to bulk carriers leads to less thorough inspections than they deserve, or none at all. Means of access have frequently proved inadequate or worse. The Bureau Veritas paper said that 'means of access need to be provided for preventative maintenance and inspection of the maximum possible amount of structure'.[5] This had to be designed into the ship as built. And this means higher costs.

But there are changes on the way. Harland and Wolff we have already mentioned. Their design, incidentally, will use a far smaller proportion of high tensile steel (about 30 per cent) and great reserves of structural strength (redundancy), particularly in the cargo spaces, sides and internals, along with an enhanced corrosion protection system. In Italy a series of three of the world's largest dry bulk carriers being built by Fincantieri have incorporated the recommendations of a special committee set up after bulk carrier losses of recent years. This committee consisted of members of the Italian shipbuilding research organisation, the owners and builders – and the classification society. Special attention was paid to areas known to be prone to fatigue, stress, corrosion and cargo damage. As a result the ship designs were altered to build in thicker shell plates in vulnerable areas, strengthening in ballast tanks, collar plates at the web frames and longitudinal connections and strengthening around the hatches and coamings.

Meanwhile, at sea, the master of the *Manila Transporter* abandoned ship in the Indian Ocean after cracks appeared in her shell plating. After 'unusual' movements detected by an increased awareness of the worldwide problem, he took the decision to get his crew off. It was assumed the ship had sunk but, some weeks later, it was found and some attempts were made to salvage it. When finally professional salvors arrived, they took one look and ran. The next day she sank.

In December 1991 the Italian-built, twenty-two-year-old bulk carrier, *Sonata*, loaded with 75,100 tonnes of iron pellets, was bound for Weserport, Germany, from Kirkenes in Norway. She sprang a leak. Tugs were called but as the salvage leader, Per Farsted, said: 'The ship suddenly keeled over with a loud noise and it is likely that the hull cracked. It took seconds before she was upside down.'

The 122,433 dwt, eighteen-year-old *Berlina* was under the coal loaders in Port Kemble, New South Wales, when cracks were discovered. She was moved off berth for more detailed examination. The ship had just passed her Norwegian classification survey and her managers insisted the damage was superficial, due to bad weather. After a week, including picketing by waterfront unions, the ship was repaired. The Australian government was, by the end of 1991, conducting investigations into bulk carrier losses, not least because of accusations over the loading techniques at Dampier.

Even so, at the start of 1992 old bulk carriers were a highly profitable form of ship to own or charter; there were almost no scrappings and very little new building. We have to say there are going to be many more casualties, many more deaths before things start to get better. This is not a happy conclusion but it is born out of the continuing failure of international shipping to put its house in order. Years of slump have not helped; the availability of good profits in the old ships will, in the absence of hard-nosed and probably local regulation, mean they will keep on sailing.

Seafarers will go on manning them too. If we examine the background to many of the crews today, this is also easy to appreciate. Going to sea used to be one way of 'bettering' yourself in this country. Today it is true of huge tracts of the Third World, especially those with a long seafaring tradition. The money sent back to grateful families, set against the chance of drowning, will continue to ensure a steady supply of desperate men from these poorer countries, willing to risk their lives to feed their families.

In the immediate future, the only chance there is to prevent dangerous ships from sailing is local port control. It has to come to that: port regulations have to be enforced to the full – and tightened considerably where they are weak. The rules should be legally binding, for ships inward and outward bound, and port authorities must be given much greater powers to seize and hold ships they deem to be unsafe.

At the same time we believe governments have to move to make classification societies much more accountable, and legally liable if they pass a ship which is subsequently shown to have been unsafe, either through loss or damage. The whole of shipping would benefit from a gale, rather than a wind, of change towards openness. If the shipping business is unwilling to do this voluntarily, it should be forced into it. Only when the books are made much more available will we see a process of change which will lead to better standards – in shipbuilding, in ship ownership and in operation.

It will, almost certainly, lead to pressure to raise prices of raw materials and finished goods. Yet the industry is prepared to allow huge sums to be paid out, year after year, in insurance. This, alongside the loss of life, has to be a nonsense. If the loss of the *Derbyshire* is to have any lasting impact on the shipping industry, it has to be here.

Those who live their lives out on the land have always found it easy to ask seafarers to go to sea, to bring us both the mundane and exotic goods we crave. We should not be mistaken, most seafarers love the life and could not easily settle on land. But if we are to go on expecting these men and women to take that road, to 'the lonely sea and sky', we have to ensure that, when they go, they do so in well-found ships, never ever again in a ship too far.

Epilogue

By the early spring of 1992, a number of developments had taken place with regard to the worldwide crisis in bulk carriers.

Lloyd's Register had issued a series of new guidelines designed to beef up the inspections made by surveyors, and encouraging masters of bulk carriers to inspect their ships more thoroughly. These guidelines had come under some criticism for their statement that ships' officers would be able to find flaws. One bulk carrier master, Michael Lloyd, pointed out in an article in *Lloyd's List*:

> A typical bulk carrier will have up to 50 frames per hatch with a depth of around 23 metres from the tank top to the top of the hold. To give this the thorough inspection suggested in the advisory 'where to look and what to look for' diagram will require as a minimum at least two officers for one day per hold.[1]

Early in 1992 Australia's two main iron ore exporters (Hamersley Iron and Broken Hill Pty) banned bulk carriers of over fifteen years from loading at her ports, a dramatic move aimed at damping down any idea that it was the loading of these ships (see Diagram 1, p. 139) which had caused so many to sink after leaving Australian ports. The Norwegian authorities, meanwhile, started compulsory inspection of Panamanian and Maltese flag bulk carriers in an attempt to reduce casualties. The inspections will also look at older vessels under other flags. The Norwegian port of Narvik is visited by around 225 bulk carriers a year.

In Britain, Malcolm Rifkind was warning the low quality registers that sub-standard ships could be banned from British ports: 'More radically, we might seek to agree with like-minded countries that vessels should be denied access to our ports if they do not meet the same standards as our own.'

He added: 'It is in our national interest to ensure that safety and environmental impact are high on the agenda when formulating shipping policy both domestically and internationally.'[2]

It was with that aim in view that a most dramatic event took place at the end of February, 1992. In an unusually hard-hitting report, the House of Lords Select Committee on Science and Technology discussed ship design and safety. We quote from the conclusions because they mirror what we have said throughout this book.

The report says, *inter alia*:

> We are aware that the inherited framework (of ship safety) may be said to have served well up till now. But things are changing: ship technology is developing faster than ever before, while risks which were often considered acceptable fifty years ago are not acceptable now . . . Shipping must not be allowed to become a victim of its own long history.

> The Committee want 'primary safety goals' (including standards of structural strength, stability) and a 'safety case' for every ship, demonstrating that the ship's operations were intimately connected to safety at all times. The Committee believed it was important to place the issue of safety firmly with the operator, rather than with the flag state, fostering a 'safety culture'.

With respect to ship science, and its place in the design of ships the Committee said:

> . . . we note the progress which ship science has made in the last twenty years, reinforced by metallurgy and computer technology . . . We acknowledge the reasons why the advance of ship science may have slowed down. The two major reasons appear to be the poor state of the shipbuilding industry during the 1980s, and the absence of any imperative to conduct forward-looking research in safety matters . . . *We urge the Government not to leave British ship science altogether to the mercy of market forces* [their emphasis].

The Committee was also exercised by the issue of steel in the building of ships:

> . . . we recommend that the classification societies should continue to press for greater selective use of steels with guaranteed fracture toughness in order to increase the critical size of cracks . . .

And they went on to recommend that

> . . . all ships over 20,000 dwt should be fitted with hull stress monitoring systems, and that voyage data recorders should become mandatory for all ships covered by the SOLAS (Safety of Life At Sea) Convention.[3]

More still, though was to come. The Committee want more inspection by Port/State control; they want more open circulation of the results of inspections to all concerned, including classification societies and insurers. Most of all they want the Surveyor General's Organisation (SGO) in the UK, part of the Department of Transport's Marine Directorate, to become an independent statutory Civil Maritime Authority (CMA) 'along the lines of the CAA (Civil Aviation Authority)' – this was actually recommended by the Rochdale Inquiry into Shipping as long ago as 1970, the year immediately before the *Derbyshire* class ships were started.

Plus ça change . . .

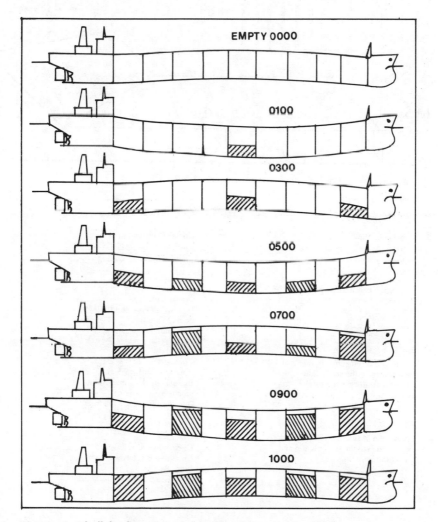

Diagram 1 A bulk loading sequence showing the stress put on bulkers

Diagram 2 Where to look and what to look for

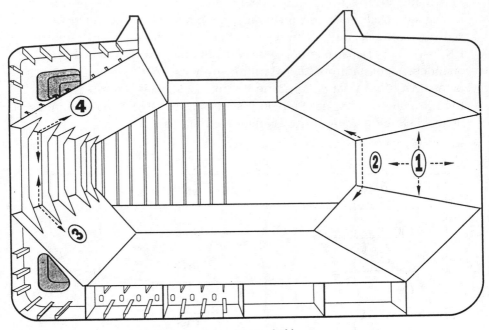

Typical cross section of bulk carrier through cargo hold.

Where to look	What to look for
① Side shell plating.	Cracks in welds or plates. Leaks in welds or plates. Distortion of plating.
② Connection of bulkhead plating to side shell.	Punctured plating. Cracked plating. Heavily indented plating. Buckled plating. Corrosion and wastage.
③ Connection of side shell frames and end brackets to the shell plating and hopperside tank plating by close-up inspection.	Cracks. Corrosion and wastage. Excessively deformed frames or brackets. Detached frames or brackets.
④ Connection of side shell frames and end brackets to the shell plating and topside tank plating.	Cracks. Corrosion and wastage. Excessively deformed frames or brackets. Detached frames or brackets.

Appendix

Furness Withy, owners of the first of the Bridge class of OBO, followed the building of their giant ship closely in their house journal, from which the following extracts are taken:

What else can we tell you about her? . . . in the unlikely event of the OBO carrying a full cargo of milk, she would discharge 312 million pintas – and still have enough over to fill the *Andes* swimming pool.

There was mention of the OBO's 'double skin' – virtually two hulls, one inside the other. The space in between these hulls will be used for water ballast. Two holds may also be used for the same purpose, and the total ballast capacity will be just short of 100,000 tons.

The stem will be fitted with a bulbous forefoot – a sausage-shaped protrusion moulded into the bow line, a feature that is now commonly used on new ships for the prime purpose of decreasing water resistance. The nine hatch covers (each 71 feet wide and between 40 and 48 feet long) are opened and closed automatically, operated by a hydraulic rack and pinion drive.

We hear a great deal these days about the speedy discharge of bulk cargoes. This is amply borne out by the fact that the OBO's three main oil pumps will between them have a discharge rate in the region of 9000 tonnes per hour.

Most of the enormous tonnage of steel reaches Teesside from mills in Lincolnshire. Piles of sections and plates lie rust-covered and blistered as the stock-pile grows outside the prefabrication shed. The metal is un-treated when it reaches the yard – hence oxidisation causes further deterioration of the surfaces, and weathering adds rust to the layer that must be removed before work can commence.

The process of shotblasting entails blasting the steel with metal shot to lift scab from the surface. Oxidisation starts again the instant the metal is exposed to the air, so immediately the shotblasting is complete the metal is coated with a primer to prevent renewed corrosion.

The steel plates are then ready for burning, rolling if necessary and then fabrication. They are carried from one part of the shed to another by gantries fitted with dozens of electromagnets. A steel plate is placed in position for burning; the acetylene cutter moves along the required pattern, piloted automatically from a control room nearby in which a light beam can be seen following the outline of the section of a 1/10th scale loftsman's drawing.

When several plates and sections are ready they are welded together into units and placed alongside the slipway, ready for erection.

How do they go about this business of erecting a ship? Most of us are aware that the hull is basically a shell strengthened at intervals with sections known as bulkheads fitted across the hull. A ship of the size and type of the OBO has a very deep double-bottom . . . this consists of the bottom shell (the very bottom part of the hull which since it is virtually flat and nearly 150 feet wide is not technically a keel) and the double-bottom itself, a labyrinthine structure about eight feet in height (slightly more towards the sides as there is an incline to allow drainage) the top of which forms the base of the cargo holds and machinery space.

Construction starts with the bottom shell and double-bottom sections, at a point approximately two-thirds aft. It then spreads upwards as well as fore and aft, as the upper sections of the hull amidships are being welded into place before the lower portions nearer the bow and stern are finished. After a length of bottom shell has been laid double-bottom sections are lowered into place on top. Temporary bars are welded across the joints to ensure that each section remains in exact position during the major welding process.

By mid-November [1969] about 60 per cent of the bottom shell was in position topped by some 25 per cent of the double-bottom, though not all of this had yet been welded. An indication of the shape was emerging. And of the size too, for the full width of the ship was visible once the first of the double-bottom hopper tanks were positioned on each side of the hull. They are the corner pieces that join the side and bottom structures; they weigh something like 60 tons each. These tanks are used for water ballast which is pumped in and out . . . Powerful spring clips maintain the hopper tanks' approximate position until the time for welding arrives.

Appendix*Appendix*

When that task is complete the bottom bulkhead stools are lifted on to the double-bottom, forming a bridge between port and starboard hopper tanks.

On to these, side-pieces were lifted, then the top corner saddle tanks – hopper tanks in reverse. At that point the full depth of the hull – 82 feet – was reached.

While the midship sections are building upwards, the forward and after areas continue with the erection of the double-bottom and hopper tanks. Already cast and lying to one side is the stern frame ready for lifting in place in due course.

The vast open tank-bottom area has been broken by two almost complete bulkheads (a third being added a few days later), some bulkhead stools, hopper tanks and a considerable amount of side-plating. The first two erected bulkheads enclose hold 7 and we are now able to stand at the bottom of the hold and look up towards what will be the main deck, towering 80 feet or so above. The various vertical structures are temporarily strengthened by a maze of wire hawsers between which we have to pick our way carefully.

The bulkheads are built up from prefabricated units which are swung into their allotted position by the dockyard cranes, then welded into place. Once two bulkheads are up, the sidewall of the ship can be erected between them and from this core the construction will spread fore and aft.

June, 1970: the speed with which ship 25 is progressing takes the uninitiated aback . . . The centre section of the hull is now totally enclosed except for the yawning mouths of the hatchways. Some of the partially completed hatch covers are lying alongside the ship. Large areas of the upper deck are in place – an enormous steel promenade littered with the organised chaos of construction.

At the stern, now being put together, the Furness Withy correspondent noted:

More decks have to be built into this section of the hull, the lower areas for various machinery installations, and later crew accommodation in the upper decks. The compartmentation in this region is thus of much smaller units than in the cargo area, explaining the complexity in design.

Already the ship's bottom is receiving a coat of anticorrosive paint. It is a strange experience wandering through the labyrinthine forest of concrete blocks and wood piles on which this enormous weight rests. To all but the technically-minded few, the way in which 24,000 tons of steel is supported on this seemingly inadequate base remains a mystery.

The *Furness Bridge* was launched on October 16th 1970 by the Duchess of Kent, the bow and stern having been fitted last. She was the biggest OBO in the world. At the time of the launch Furness Withy chairman, John MacConochie, said the building of the ship was 'an act of faith'. How right he was.

Sir John Hunter, chairman of Swan Hunter, said: 'Britain's greatness was founded on her ships and the skills and labours of her shipbuilders who built them. It would be a sorry day for this country if her merchant navy were ever allowed to decline or the shipbuilding skills necessary to provide its continuance and enhancement permitted to decay.' He was speaking, of course, at the Haverton Hill yard.

Notes

The authors are grateful to owners of copyrights for kind permission to use quotations from printed works, private letters and interviews; and also for private photographs used as illustrations.

1   The Last Hours of the Derbyshire

1   Lloyd's Report: from the *Department of Transport Factual Statement on the loss of the* Derbyshire, May 1981.
2   MV *Derbyshire*: Report of Court, No. 8075, Formal Investigation (HMSO, 1989).

2   A Theory on the Loss of the Derbyshire

1   'A Theory on the Loss of the MV *Derbyshire*.' Royal Institute of Naval Architects paper, read on October 18, 1990 (RINA paper).

3   Decline and Fall: British Shipping 1970–1990

1   *British Shipping: Challenges and Opportunities.* Report by a joint working party chaired by the Secretary of State for Transport and the President of the General Council of British Shipping (HMSO, 1990).
2   Ibid.
3   Issued by African Wharfage Co. Ltd, Stevedores, East African Ports.
4   Thomas's *Stowage* (Brownson & Ferguson, 1983).
5   'Decline of the UK registered merchant fleet'. *First report of the Transport Committee, House of Commons (Session 1987–8).*
6   See Glossary.
7   British Maritime Charitable Foundation. *Why the Ships Went* (1989).

4   A Family Tragedy

1   Dave Ramwell's article appeared in *Sea Breezes* in June 1989.

5 *The Bridge Class of Ships: a family of woes*

1   MV *Derbyshire*, Report of Court, op. cit.
2   RINA paper, op. cit.
3   Ibid.
4   Peter Ridyard correspondence.
5   Ibid.
6   Ibid.
7   1985 Draft Report of the *Report into the circumstances attending the loss of MV Derbyshire*. Department of Transport, July 1985.
8   Ibid.
9   Ibid.
10 Ibid.
11 RINA paper, op. cit.
12 Lloyd's Report, Rotterdam, no. 200768, 1982.
13 Ibid.
14 RINA paper, op. cit., quoting Lloyd's Report, Piraeus, no. 700308, 1990.

6   *A Deepening Mystery*

1   MV *Derbyshire*: Report of Court, op. cit.
2   *Factual Statement*, op. cit.
3   Ibid.
4   Ibid.
5   RINA paper, op. cit.
6   *Factual Statement*, op. cit.
7   Ibid.
8   *Observer*, January 9, 1989.
9   Ibid.
10 Ibid.
11 Ibid.
12 Draft Report, op. cit.
13 Ibid.
14 Ibid.
15 Ibid.
16 Ibid.
17 Ibid.
18 Ibid.
19 *Final Report of the circumstances surrounding the loss of MV Derbyshire*, March 1986.
20 Ibid.
21 Ibid.
22 Ibid.
23 Ibid.
24 Ibid.
25 Ibid.
26 Ibid.

7   The Detective: framing the evidence

1   Ridyard correspondence.
2   Ibid.
3   Ibid.
4   Ibid.
5   Ibid.
6   Ibid.
7   Ibid.

8   The Ship that Died of Shame

1   *Daily Telegraph* reports, November 24, 1986.
2   Letter to Dave Ramwell.
3   RINA paper, op. cit.
4   Ibid.

9   Hardening Truths

1   Draft Report, op. cit.
2   Ibid.
3   Ibid.
4   Ibid.
5   Ibid.
6   Ibid.
7   RINA paper, op. cit.
8   Ibid.
9   Ibid.
10   Ibid.
11   Ibid.
12   Ibid.
13   Ibid.
14   Ibid.
15   Ibid.

10   How the Ships were Built

1   MV *Derbyshire* Report of Court, op. cit.
2   Ibid.
3   Transcript of Formal Inquiry hearing.
4   Ibid.
5   Ibid.
6   Ibid.
7   Ibid.
8   Ibid.

9   Ibid.
10   Ibid.
11   MV *Derbyshire* Report of Court, op. cit.
12   Transcript of Formal Inquiry hearings.

12   Petition in Parliament

1   Letter from Eddie Loyden to Patrick Macloughlin, November 9, 1989.
2   Written reply from Patrick Macloughlin to Eddie Loyden, November 10, 1989.
3   Hansard, May 1986.
4   Hansard, October 1990.
5   Ibid.

13   Losses in Bulk

1   *Lloyd's List*, editorial, September 17, 1991.
2   Ibid. October 15, 1991.
3   Eric Beetham: 'Loss of Bulk Carriers', *Seaways*, May 1991.
4   Captain Lanham, Letters, *Seaways*, September 1991.
5   Mr Brooking, Letters, *Seaways*, August 1991.
6   John Ferguson: 'Bulk Carriers – The Challenge', *Seaways*, August 1991.
7   'Vanishing Bulkers: a special report', *Lloyd's List*, September 1991.
8   Ibid.
9   *Lloyd's List*, editorial, October 1991.

14   Time for Change

1   *Fairplay International*, December 6, 1990.
2   *Seven Seas*, BBC World Service, November 22, 1991.
3   Trans-Alaska Pipeline Service (TAPS); Tanker Structural Failure Study, published by the US Coastguard in June 1990.
4   *Lloyd's List*, September 17, 1991.
5   Ibid.

Epilogue

1   *Lloyd's List*, January 22, 1992.
2   NUMAST *Telegraph*, February 1992.
3   Report of the House of Lords Select Committee on Science and Technology, February 1992.

Glossary

BOTTOM SLAMMING occurs when the ship lifts out of the water forward and being thus unsupported, slams down heavily on the surface.

BRITTLE FRACTURE occurs when the metal fractures suddenly and leaves clean edges with little or no distortion of the metal adjacent to the crack. It is usually associated with poor quality metal and low temperatures, i.e. the lower the temperature the greater the likelihood of brittle fracture. Very little energy is expended in a brittle fracture. Crudely it could be considered like glass breaking. A brittle fracture travels *very* fast.

A **BULKHEAD** is a partition in a ship which forms separate compartments. Those placed fore and aft are longitudinal bulkheads; those placed athwartships (i.e. across the ship) are transverse bulkheads.

A **COFFERDAM** is the watertight space between two bulkheads.

DOUBLE BOTTOMS are compartments formed at the bottom of a ship by plating over the girder arrangements which are attached to the inner bottom plating. They are often used for carrying water ballast and enhance safety in the event of the ship's bottom being holed.

DOUBLE SKIN CONSTRUCTION refers to the creation, during construction, of a cavity between the ship's side plating and the hold (rather like a cavity wall in a house). This lends some strength to the ship and serves as additional protection should the outer shell plating be punctured in any way.

A **DOUBLING PLATE** (or **'DOUBLER'**) is a piece of plate welded over another plate to effect a repair (if, say, the underneath plate is holed) or to lend strength. In this book the term has also been employed to describe those plates used to close gaps where a longitudinal member fails to reach the bulkhead it is supposed to meet. Some surveyors have also used the word PAD for the same thing.

HATCH COAMING This is the 'wall' around a hold upon which the hatch covers are placed.

A **HOG** occurs when the vessel is supported only in the middle causing it to droop at either end. Heavy loads fore and aft with little in the middle can also hog a ship.

KEEL This is the general construction built on and including the longitudinal bottom centre plate of the ship; for example a single girder attached to the bottom plate internally at 90 degrees to it would form a 'flat plate keel', whereas two girders would form a 'duct keel'.

NOTCH TOUGHNESS When toughness of metal is to be tested a sample bar of the metal is cut with a 'V' notch across one face; it is clamped just below the notch and then struck above the notch by a swinging pendulum (of kinetic energy 120 ft/lb). After hitting and fracturing the notched bar it continues to swing through an arc that is then measured to indicate the work done to cause fracture. This then is the notch toughness of the metal.

A **PAD** is usually taken to be a piece of reinforcing metal attached to a bulkhead to help distribute otherwise concentrated stresses.

A **SAG** occurs when a ship is supported at either end but not in the middle. Heavy cargo in the middle with little fore and aft may produce a sag.

SCANTLINGS are the dimensions of the individual parts which make up a ship.

A **SCARPH** is a form of joint, usually for the larger parts of a ship's members. A **SCARPHING PIECE** is a specially fabricated piece that joins members in such a way as to avoid concentrations of stresses.

SHELL PLATING is the collective term for all the plates attached to the frames; they make up the sides of the ship.

SPURLING PIPE This is the pipe which carries the anchor cable from the windlass (which winds it in) down into the anchor cable locker where the cable is stowed. Similarly when the anchor is let go it drags the cable out of the locker via the spurling pipe.

TONNAGE MEASUREMENTS Confusion is easy. A merchant ship, for instance, might have tonnages listed of 10,000, 7500, 3000, 5200 and 3500. This is possible because quite different things are measured. For one thing, 'tons' can mean weight or the equivalence in weight to 100 cubic feet of enclosed space.
Displacement tonnage: This is the total weight of a ship and everything on board. Never normally used for merchant ships, this is the standard way of describing the size of warships.

Deadweight tonnage: This is the weight of all the cargo, stores and fuel carried by a ship when fully loaded (to her marks). It is the displacement tonnage less the weight of the ship (her lightweight tonnage). It is the best indication of her earning capacity (and lift).

Gross registered tonnage: This is the total *cubic* capacity of all enclosed space at 100 cubic feet to the ton. Used for maritime registers.

Net registered tonnage: The same as for gross tonnage but the total space less engine room, crew accommodation, stores and so on. It is a measure of the *earning* space of a ship.

TORQUE is the force which causes torsion when it is applied in equal and opposite manner, each end of the hull.

TORSION refers to a twisting movement – more likely to happen with long ships' hulls.

TRAMPING is the practice of going wherever the shipper desires rather than following any regular route.

UPPER AND LOWER HOPPER TANKS would best be expressed as the wing tanks at the upper and lower parts of the hold (or hopper).

VEEING OUT is the practice of chamfering plate edges to be welded so that there is an angle of about 60 degrees between them. A 'V' shaped gulley is thus formed along which the welding runs are made to join the plates.

WING TANKS are tanks situated at the ship's sides.

Index

Kowloon Bridge (previously *English Bridge*), 39, 41, 46, 51, 69, 110; abandoned, 72; Bishop, Price research links with *Derbyshire*, 17; crew taken off, 71; film of, 107, 114; and Frame 65, 13, 62, 74, 75, 109; Lloyd's Report, 74–5; loss triggers off inquiry, 75, 100, 103, 105, 107, 110; not remodified, 62, 70, 107; oil spillage, 73; Reo considers unseaworthy, 70–1; sinks, 13, 62, 72–5, 100
Kyushu, 8

Labour government, and grant scheme, 19, 24, 82
Lake Arrowhead, 68
Lambert, Paul, 37, 113–14
Lambert, Peter, 37
Lanham, Captain, 124–5
Leak, Gerald, 85
Lean, Geoffrey, 54
Leatherbarrow, Ted, 116
Liberia, 20
Liberian Deputy Commissioner of Maritime Affairs, 58
lifeboats, 5, 9, 34–5, 52, 53, 67, 106, 131
liner trade, 23, 25
Liverpool, 3, 5, 12, 35, 37, 46, 51, 112, 113, 115
Liverpool Bridge (later *Derbyshire*), 4, 39, 46, 61, 114
Liverpool Cathedral, 12, 34
Liverpool Mission to Seamen, 18
Lloyd, Michael, 137
Lloyd's List, 61, 118, 126, 129, 137
Lloyd's Register Executive Board, 44
Lloyd's Register of Shipping, 64, 67; barristers at inquiry, 103, 109; Bridge class building, 86, 87–8; and BSRA, 58; and certificates for *Derbyshire*, 54; changes methods of survey for bulkers, 117; *Derbyshire* insurance settlement, 10; and *Derbyshire* surveys, 5; examines *East Bridge*, 73; financial implications of growing losses of bulk carriers, 7;

and Frame 65, 47, 61, 65, 73, 110; *Kowloon Bridge* report, 74–5; and loading alternate holds, 84; and misalignment, 95; modification in Bridge class 'approved', 105; research division, 61; sees itself as the best classification society and rule maker, 132; ship design changes mislaid, xi, xii, 58–9, 69, 88; and shipping finance, 133; and steel grades, 44; and strain gauges, 79; surveyor's reply to Bishop, Price research, 15, 17; and Swan Hunter Standards Book, 90; and *Tyne Bridge*, 42, 43, 44; welding rules, 89
Lloyd's Underwriters, 60
load lines, 18
loading, 120–3, 125, 126, 127, 132, 137
lobbies, 19–20, 28, 29
Loyden, Eddie, 112–16
Luzon Strait, 53

McAlenan, Eric, 116
McDowell, Mr (surveyor), 123–4
McGrath, Peter, 116
McLoughlin, Patrick, 113, 126
MacNeill, H., 67
Madge, Tim, xii–xiii, 18
Mallam, Douglas, 85
Malmö, Sweden, 89
Malta, 137
Manila Transporter, 134–5
Marcona Pathfinder (previously *Furness Bridge*), 39, 65, 68
Marine Accident Investigation Branch (MAIB), 113
marine engine research, 25
Marine Institute, 130
Marine Society, 28
Marriott, Captain Peter, 17, 122
mates, and loading of mixed cargo, 22
Maudsley Hospital, London, 34
Melbourne, 23
merchant fleet: decline of, 19, 28–30; deep-sea, 28–30; flight from the British register, 20, 26–7, 28, 30; requisition of ships in Falklands